AN OUTLINE OF ENGLISH PRONUNCIATION

Undervisningsmateriale fra
Institut for Sprog og Kommunikation
Syddansk Universitet

Niels Davidsen-Nielsen

AN OUTLINE OF ENGLISH PRONUNCIATION

Translated and Revised
by
Fritz Larsen & Hans Frede Nielsen

UNIVERSITY PRESS OF SOUTHERN DENMARK
2008

© The author and Odense University Press 1994
Second revised edition 1997
Third revised edition 2000
Second impression 2008
Printed by Narayana Press, Denmark
Cover design by Ulla Poulsen Precht
ISBN 978-87-7838-552-9

CONTENTS

PREFACE   7

LIST OF SYMBOLS USED   9

1. INTRODUCTORY   11
    1.1. The communication process and the three branches of phonetics   11
    1.2. The organs of speech   11

2. PRONUNCIATION AND LANGUAGE   17
    2.1. The linguistic hierarchy   17
    2.2. The phoneme   18
    2.3. Distinctive features   19

3. APPLIED PHONETICS   23

4. SOUND AND WRITING IN ENGLISH   27

5. THE ENGLISH CONSONANTS   29
    5.1. Vowels and consonants   29
    5.2. The inventory of consonant phonemes   30
    5.3. The system of consonants   31
    5.4. Comparison with Danish   33
    5.5. The release stage of stops   35
    5.6. The distinction between voiced and voiceless stops   37
    5.7. A comparison between English and Danish stops   39
    5.8. The stop phonemes   40
    5.9. The distinction between voiced and voiceless fricatives   46
    5.10. The fricative phonemes   47
    5.11. The nasals   55
    5.12. The liquids   57
    5.13. The semi-vowels   59

6. THE ENGLISH VOWELS   63
    6.1. Description of the vowels   63
    6.2. The inventory of vowel phonemes   65
    6.3. The system of vowels   66
    6.4. Comparison with Danish   68
    6.5. Vowel length   69
    6.6. The long monophthongs   71
    6.7. The short monophthongs   75

- 6.8. The diphthongs   83
- 6.9. Vowels in unaccented syllables   90

7. ENGLISH PROSODY   97
   - 7.1. Introductory remarks on accent   97
   - 7.2. The English accentual system   99
   - 7.3. Accent in polysyllabic words   100
   - 7.4. Accent in compounds   104
   - 7.5. Sentence accent and rhythm   107
   - 7.6. Introductory remarks on intonation   110
   - 7.7. The tone group   113
   - 7.8. The classification of tone groups   116
   - 7.9. Comparison with Danish   118
   - 7.10. Simplified transcription   123
   - 7.11. The use of the tone-group types   125
   - 7.12. Connected tone groups   131
   - 7.13. Intonation and syntax   134

8. SOUND COMBINATIONS   139
   - 8.1. Assimilation   139
   - 8.2. The English syllable   141

ANNOTATED BIBLIOGRAPHY   143

APPENDIX
   Table 1: English consonants   149
   Table 2: English monophthongs   150

INDEX   151

PREFACE

Translators' preface

The present volume is a revised translation of the second editon of Niels Davidsen-Nielsen, *Engelsk udtale i hovedtræk* (Copenhagen: Gyldendal, 1983). The immediate occasion for publishing an English version of the book is that some time ago the English Department at Odense University decided to make English the language of instruction in all courses offered by the Department. As we have used the Danish version as a set book in our British English phonetics classes since 1985, it was only natural that the idea of translating it into English should present itself. We would like to stress that our endeavours have been aimed at translating (and where necessary, revising) the book, not at writing a new phonetics book. For pedagogical reasons we have chosen to include cardinal vowel diagrams in the articulary descriptions of the English vowels, diagrams originally published in Niels Davidsen-Nielsen, *Engelsk fonetik* (Copenhagen: Gyldendal, 1970) but in several cases revised by us.

Our warmest thanks are due to the following colleagues for their useful comments and advice: Niels Hald (Århus), Arne Juul (Frederiksberg), Hanne Lauridsen (Copenhagen), Inger Mees (Copenhagen), Sharon Millar (Odense), Francis Nolan (Cambridge) and Torben Vestergaard (Aalborg). We are also very grateful to Niels Davidsen-Nielsen for his cooperation and support during the whole process of translating and revising the volume. We are indebted to Helle Kit Rasmussen for all the care she has taken in producing the camera-ready typescript and to Inger Bjerg Poulsen for preparing or redrawing the illustrations of the book. Finally, we would like to thank the Institute of Language and Communication at Odense University for supporting this project in numerous ways.

Fritz Larsen
Hans Frede Nielsen

Author's preface

In recent years it has become common practice in departments of English in Denmark to use English as a language of instruction in all courses, including phonetics and grammar. This is a change I welcome and have advocated myself. There is, therefore, now a need for textbook material in English and I am pleased that it was decided at Odense University to translate *Engelsk udtale i hovedtræk* into English. I could wish for nobody better qualified for this piece of work than Fritz Larsen and Hans Frede Nielsen. As my Danish book in its second, revised edition dates back to 1983, it has been necessary for them to revise it on a number of points, particularly to take recent developments in English pronunciation into account. I am very grateful to Fritz Larsen and Hans Frede Nielsen for undertaking the difficult and time-consuming task of translating and revising my book. Finally, it gives me pleasure that it is produced at Odense University, which I have had specially close contacts with since the late sixties.

Niels Davidsen-Nielsen
Department of English
Copenhagen Business School

LIST OF SYMBOLS USED

Consonants

/p/ as in *pie* /paɪ/	/s/ as in *sigh* /saɪ/
/b/ - - *buy* /baɪ/	/z/ - - *Zoo* /zu:/
/t/ - - *tie* /taɪ/	/ʃ/ - - *shy* /ʃaɪ/
/d/ - - *die* /daɪ/	/ʒ/ - - *rouge* /ru:ʒ/
/tʃ/ - - *chew* /tʃu:/	/h/ - - *high* /haɪ/
/dʒ/ - - *Jew* /dʒu:/	/m/ - - *my* /maɪ/
/k/ - - *coo* /ku:/	/n/ - - *nigh* /naɪ/
/g/ - - *guy* /gaɪ/	/ŋ/ - - *pang* /pæŋ/
/f/ - - *fie* /faɪ/	/l/ - - *lie* /laɪ/
/v/ - - *vie* /vaɪ/	/r/ - - *rye* /raɪ/
/θ/ - - *thigh* /θaɪ/	/w/ - - *why* /waɪ/
/ð/ - - *thy* /ðaɪ/	/j/ - - *you* /ju:/

Vowels

Monophthongs
/i:/ as in *heed* /hi:d/
/ɪ/ - - *hid* /hɪd/
/e/ - - *head* /hed/
/æ/ - - *had* /hæd/
/ɑ:/ - - *hard* /hɑ:d/
/ɒ/ - - *hod* /hɒd/
/ɔ:/ - - *hoard* /hɔ:d/
/ʊ/ - - *hood* /hʊd/
/u:/ - - *hoot* /hu:t/
/ə/ - - *paper* /'peɪpə/
/ɜ:/ - - *hurt* /hɜ:t/
/ʌ/ - - *hut* /hʌt/

Diphthongs
/eɪ/ as in *hate* /heɪt/
/aɪ/ - - *height* /haɪt/
/ɔɪ/ - - *boy* /bɔɪ/
/əʊ/ - - *go* /gəʊ/
/aʊ/ - - *how* /haʊ/
/ɪə/ - - *hear* /hɪə/
/eə/ - - *hair* /heə/
/ʊə/ - - *pure* /pjʊə/

:   indicates that the preceding vowel is long, cf. [hɑ:t] (*heart*).
'   indicates that the following syllable is accented, cf. [fə'get] (*forget*).
˳   placed under or over a letter, this symbol signifies devoicing as in [kl̥aɪm] (*climb*) and [li:g̊] (*league*).
ˌ   placed under or over a consonant letter, this symbol signifies syllabicity as in ['bætl̩] (*battle*) and ['beɪkn̩] (*bacon*).

[ ]   square brackets are used for enclosing speech sounds.
/ /   slashes are used for enclosing phonemes.
ʔ   denotes a glottal plosive.
ɫ   indicates that /l/ is velarised as in [bɔːɫ] (*ball*).

1. INTRODUCTORY

1.1. The communication process and the three branches of phonetics

The communication between two human beings, A and B, is the result of a complicated process, which can be summarized in the following manner:

1. The message that A wishes to transmit is linguistically encoded in his brain.
2. Via the nervous system instructions are sent from the speech centre of A's brain to his organs of speech.
3. A's organs of speech begin to move.
4. The movement of A's speech organs produces sound waves that are propagated in all directions.
5. Some of the sound waves reach B's ear drum and are conducted from here to his middle ear and then to his internal ear.
6. The nerve impulses from B's internal ear are received by the auditory centre of his brain.
7. These impulses are decoded in B's brain: they are interpreted linguistically.

It should be noted that A is both speaker and listener. The sound waves also reach his own ears, enabling him to utilize the acoustic information for constantly correcting his own speech activity. This feedback mechanism is a control measure of considerable importance, cf. the speech difficulties of the deaf.

Since relatively little is known of the activity that takes place in the human brain and in the nervous system, phonetic science is primarily concerned with stages 3, 4 and 5 above. Phonetics can therefore be said to comprise three branches: an *articulatory*, an *acoustic* and an *auditory* branch dealing with, respectively, the movement of speech organs, the propagation of sound waves and the reception of sound (hearing). Acoustic phonetics is a discipline of scientific rather than practical interest and will therefore not be further discussed in the present book. Articulatory and auditory phonetics, on the other hand, will both be treated here, the former especially in our description of sound segments and the latter in our discussion of prosodic phenomena such as intonation and accent.

1.2. The organs of speech

The organs used for speech production are the lungs, the muscles controlling the respiratory movement, the bronchial tubes, the windpipe, the larynx, the pharynx, the mouth and the nose. The primary functions of these organs have always been biologically determined and, paradoxically, it might therefore be argued that there are *no* organs of speech. They are all part of the respiratory system. In addition, the mouth and the pharynx constitute the top part of the alimentary canal, the nose is a sense-organ of smell and the larynx acts as a valve that controls entry into the windpipe.

In the production of most sounds the organs of speech function in a manner comparable to that of a reed instrument, for instance a clarinet. In a reed instrument one or two reeds will vibrate when air is blown in, the vibrations being transmitted to the inner part of the instrument, which functions as a resonator. Similarly, the production of speech presupposes a *source of energy*, a *vibrator* and a *resonator*.

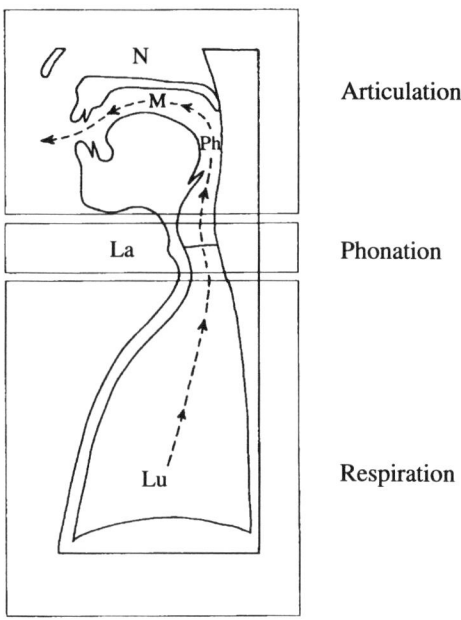

The speech mechanism: La: larynx; Lu: lungs; M: mouth; N: nose; Ph: pharynx

The source of energy is (as in the case of the reed instrument) the air-stream expelled from the lungs, the vibrator is the vocal cords in the larynx, and the resonator is the cavities in the pharynx, mouth and nose. These cavities can be modified in numerous ways and are therefore capable of producing many different types of sound quality. The human speech mechanism is thus a combination of three main systems: *respiration*, *phonation* and *articulation*.

The *respiratory system* consists of the organs of the respiratory tract: lungs, bronchial tubes, windpipe and muscles controlling the expulsion of air. In the production of speech its primary function is to provide lung air. This takes place more or less in the same way as normal exhalation and speech has therefore been called *modified breathing*. The only difference is that the exhalation is of somewhat longer duration and that its last phase is muscularly provoked and not due to a relaxation of the muscles controlling inhalation as is typical of normal breathing. In other words, in the production of speech, the respiratory system functions as a pair of bellows that sucks in air when the handles are drawn apart and squeezes air out again once the handles are pressed together.

The *phonation system* comprises the upper enlarged part of the windpipe, the larynx, whose forward portion (called the Adam's apple) is prominent in men. The inside of the larynx, which consists mainly of cartilages, has two folds of muscle stretching from front to back which jut out like shelves from the side walls of the larynx. These folds of muscle are known as the *vocal cords* and the opening between them, through which the lung air passes, is called the *glottis*. Cartilages and vocal cords can move by means of a complex set of muscles. If the vocal cords are tightened and brought close together, they vibrate when lung air passes through the glottis. *Phonation*, then, consists in the vibrations thus produced. There is phonation involved in by far the largest portion of connected speech. No English word, for instance, is formed entirely without vibration of the vocal cords, and in an utterance like *The Danes were all gorging their veal over-greedily* there is continuous vibration. However, the vibrator of the human speech mechanism is often interrupted, and this happens whenever the vocal cords move away from each other. An English word like *seal*, for example, diverges from *zeal* by the non-vibration of the vocal cords in the first speech sound. Voiceless sounds like [s], [θ], [p] and [k] are formed without any vibrator; instead these sounds consist in the noise arising when the air-stream from the lungs meets obstructions in the oral cavity. Since all speech sounds are either voiced or voiceless, the larynx can show two main positions which are linguistically relevant: *vibrating* and *open*. But it should be noted that the glottis can also be *closed*, and that in some languages glottal closing/opening constitutes a specific speech sound. Such a sound is attested in many types of English, and it may also characterize the Danish phenomenon called *stød*.

Voice is always closely connected with *pitch*. If the vocal cords are tightened when phonation takes place, the frequency of vibration is increased, and this entails a higher level of pitch. Conversely, a relaxation of the vocal cords will reduce the frequency of vibration and lower the pitch level. In connected speech the pitch level varies incessantly, and it is these changing patterns of pitch that we call intonation, and which are important for accentuation and the segmentation of speech. The larynx has thus two main functions: to produce voice and pitch.

The *articulatory system* comprises the *pharynx*, the *mouth* and the *nose*, which together can be said to constitute the *speech channel*. Beginning our description with the roof of the mouth, there is a ridge just behind the upper teeth which is referred to as the *alveolar ridge*. Immediately behind this is the *hard palate* and at the back is the *soft palate*, which is also called the *velum*. The surface of the tongue can be divided into four anatomically arbitrary sections corresponding to our division of the roof of the mouth. The extremity, placed just below the upper teeth, is the *tip of the tongue*, behind which lies the *blade* opposite the alveolar ridge. Facing the hard palate lies the *front* and behind this the *back of the tongue* below the soft palate. (In our description of vowels we also require the term *centre of the tongue*, which denotes the part of the tongue lying opposite the transitional area between the soft and the hard palate.) In normal breathing the air can escape from the pharynx through the nasal passage, but in speech the velum may be raised and form a closure against the pharyngeal wall.

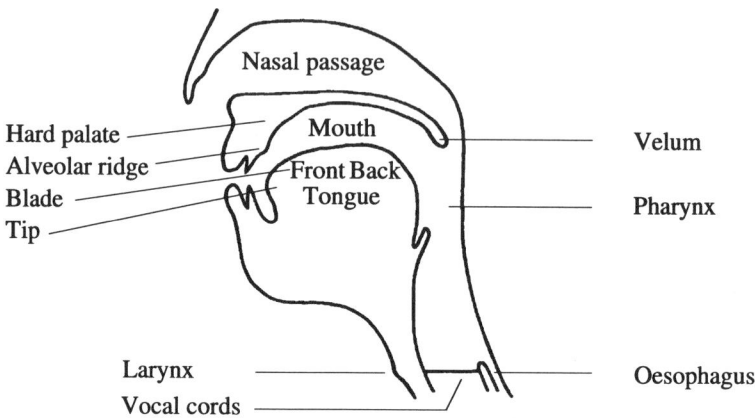

Different speech sounds can be produced by means of different *manners of articulation*. Some sounds are produced with *closure* in the oral cavity, which completely cuts off the air-stream. After a short while an explosive release of the closure takes place, and the compressed air escapes accompanied by noise. Examples of such plosives are [p], [t] and [k] in English *pin*, *tin* and *kin*. In another group of sounds the obstruction made in the oral cavity only represents a narrowing that does not interrupt the airflow, but which constitutes a stricture so close that the air-stream passes through it with *friction*. The fricatives [f] and [z] as in English *fine* and *zero* are instances of this type of articulation. A third category of speech sounds shows *approximation* between two organs in the speech channel, for example between part of the tongue and part of the palate, which is not close enough for friction to arise, but which can nevertheless decide the sound quality. This manner of articulation is especially characteristic of vowels. The degree of approximation can vary, and accordingly we operate with four distinctions: close, half close, half open and open vowels (cf. [iː], [ɪ], [e] and [æ] in English *bead*, *bid*, *bed* and *bad*). Finally, there is a class of speech sounds in which the air escapes through the nose. This class of sounds, which can be said to show *nasality*, can be exemplified by [m] and [n] in English *might* and *night*.

Another important factor contributing to differences of sound quality in speech sounds is *place of articulation*. The difference between for instance English [p], [t] and [k] consists in closures at three different points (lips, alveolar ridge and velum). The place of articulation of a speech sound is the point in the speech channel exhibiting the greatest degree of narrowing (we leave out of account the velar passage to the nose). Any type of articulation always involves two organs, a movable one called the *active articulator* and a static one known as the *passive articulator*. The most important active articulators are the lower lip and the tip, blade, front and back of the tongue. Among the passive articulators the chief ones are the upper lip, the upper teeth, the alveolar ridge and the hard and the soft palate. In accordance with this classification, we speak of labial, dental, alveolar, palatal and velar sounds. Usually the articulation occurs between organs which in neutral position lie opposite each other, for instance between the back of the tongue and the soft palate. But sometimes *displaced articulation* takes place, cf. one American English pronunciation of [r] in *right*, where the tip of the tongue shows retroflexion, being held in a position near to the hard palate.

2. PRONUNCIATION AND LANGUAGE

2.1. The linguistic hierarchy

Every language has units that belong to different linguistic levels, and which normally differ in size. An illustration of this can be given by segmenting an extensive linguistic sequence such as a *sentence* into smaller and hierarchically lower units. Let us exemplify such a linguistic analysis by means of the sentence

The tall girls accepted the present joyfully.

The first step in our linguistic analysis will be to segment this sentence into two *phrases*: *The tall girls* and *accepted the present joyfully*, which represent the immediate constituents of the sentence (subject and predicate). On the basis of their internal relations the two constituents can be divided into smaller sentence units, but this will not be discussed in this book.

By completing our sentence analysis we reach the *word* level (*the*, *tall*, *girls*, *accepted*, *present*, *joyfully*). Like sentences and phrases, words are *meaningful* units. All the words in our sentence are *commutable*, i.e. they can be replaced by other linguistic units so that changes of meaning take place; *girls*, for instance, can be replaced by *boys*, *present* by *book*, and *joyfully* by *ruefully*.

It is possible to continue our linguistic segmentation beyond the word level and arrive at even smaller meaningful sequences called *morphemes*:

The + tall + girl + s + accept + ed + the + present + joy + ful + ly.

The word *accepted* thus consists of two morphemes, *accept* and *-ed*. The sound sequence /ək'sept/ means 'take willingly', and the content of the sound sequence /-ɪd/ is 'past'. Similarly, the word *girls* can be divided into the morphemes *girl* ('female child') and *-s* ('plural'), and *joyfully* into *joy* ('feeling of happiness'), *ful* (adjectival suffix with positive connotations) and *ly* (adverbial suffix). Like words, morphemes are commutable; in addition, they can be characterized as the smallest units that have a meaning of their own. In our sentence, it is possible to substitute *less* for *full*, which would bring about a change from *joyfully* to *joylessly*.

But we are able to proceed even further with our linguistic analysis. The morpheme *girl* can be segmented into three sound units, /g/, /ɜː/ and /l/, which are all commutable. A replacement of, for example, /g/ by /h/ would change *girl* to *hurl*; if we substitute /ʌ/ for /ɜː/, the result would be *gull*; and a replacement of /l/ by /d/ would result in *gird*. These, the smallest commutable linguistic units, are called *phonemes* and are conventionally placed between slashes. It should be noted that the phoneme is a contrastive unit which has no meaning of its own (unless it functions also as a morpheme such as /z/ in /gɜːlz/). In other words, phonemes have no semantic content as such; for the time being, we can define them as the smallest contrastive linguistic units.

2.2. The phoneme

Our definition of phonemes as the smallest contrastive linguistic units should be considered a first step towards understanding what the phoneme is essentially about. In the following, we shall discuss the further implications of this concept, which takes up a position of such central importance in phonetics.

In order to establish whether two speech sounds (speech sounds are conventionally placed between brackets) represent different phonemes, we must apply the *commutation test*: in turn the two speech sounds are inserted in a phonetic sequence which constitutes a word in combination with the sound added, and the speech sounds constitute phonemes if a change of meaning takes place. If we wish to examine whether, for instance, [p] and [b] are different phonemes in English, we may add them to the phonetic sequence [-ɪn], which shows that they are in fact phonemic entities seeing that the replacement of one sound by the other results in semantic change: [pɪn] (*pin*) and [bɪn] (*bin*) have different meanings. In this case the commutation test has had a positive outcome, /p/ and /b/ having been shown to be different phonemes in English. If again we wish to examine if, for example, [ɹ] (frictionless *r* articulated with the tip of the tongue) and [r] (trill *r* articulated with the tip of the tongue) are independent phonemes in English, we may insert them in the phonetic sequence [-ɒŋ]. Here the commutation test has a negative result, however, in that there will not be any change of meaning no matter which of the two sounds is being used (in both cases the word *wrong* will be construed). The difference of sound is likely to be perceived as regional or stylistic variation but not as a distinction that is semantically relevant. Whereas /p/ and /b/ thus exhibit commutation, this is not the case with [ɹ] and [r]. Pairs of words (such as *pin* and *bin*) which diverge only with regard to one phoneme are called *minimal pairs*. For the purpose of establishing the phonemic inventory of a language, instead of using pairs, it is more practical to operate with whole series of words that are minimally different. This can be illustrated by the series *pill, till, kill, bill, dill, gill, mill, nil, fill, sill, hill, rill, will*, which shows us that /p, t, k, b, d, g, m, n, f, s, h, r, w/ are different phonemes in English.

It should be borne in mind that there can be noticeably different realisations of the same phoneme. A case in point is the divergent realisations of /k/ in the words *keep* and *coop*. The first has a forward articulation near the hard palate brought about by the following front vowel, and this gives [k] an auditory impression of being clear and high. In *coop* the back vowel following /k/ has the effect that the consonant is articulated further back (on the velum), which gives the listener an impression of this [k] as being dark and deep. It is easy to produce the two types of [k] in isolation if, when pronouncing the words, one stops immediately before the vowels are uttered. One [k] will be coloured by [i:] and the other by [u:]. The two [k] realisations are phonetically clearly different and yet they belong to the same phoneme, the reason being, of course, that they do not function as contrastive units since they never appear in the same phonetic contexts.

The different realisations of a phoneme are called *allophones* or allophonic variants. In *keep* and *coop* we saw that the two allophones of /k/ were conditioned by different phonetic environments, and in such cases we therefore speak of *conditioned* allophones. In the pronunciation of *wrong*, on the other hand, frictionless and trill *r* were not conditioned by different contexts. Realisations of this type are therefore called *free* allophonic variants, which suggests that the speaker is free to choose between two or more possible variants. The expression 'free allophonic variation' refers to both the different realisations of a given phoneme observable in different speakers and the allophonic variation that can be perceived in the speech of a single speaker on different occasions.

The concrete manifestations of a given phoneme can thus be exposed to both free and conditioned variation. If we look at allophonic variation from a somewhat different angle, it will be clear that conditioned allophones mutually exclude each other: they have a *complementary distribution*. We have seen that for instance the high, clear [k] allophone (*keep*) occurred only in contexts where the deep, dark allophone (*coop*) did not appear, and these two allophonic variants of /k/ therefore have a complementary distribution. The same applies to the three allophones of the vowel phoneme /i:/ in the series *bead*, *beat*, *bean*, which are mutually exclusive. In *bead* the vowel is relatively long; in *beat* it is perceptibly shorter; and in *bean* it is frequently partly nasalised. The three allophones, which are conditioned by three different phonetic contexts (a following voiced, voiceless or nasal consonant), can thus be said to have a complementary distribution.

But although different allophones of a phoneme can be noticeably different as we saw above, such allophones will always show a degree of phonetic similarity. Despite their phonetic divergences the two allophonic variants of the /k/ phoneme share a number of features: they are both formed by a closure made between the back of the tongue and the palate, by the soft palate shutting off the passage to the nasal cavity, and by an open glottis. Similarly, the three [i:] sounds in *bead*, *beat* and *bean* have the following characteristics in common: the front of the tongue is raised markedly towards the hard palate, and the lips are spread (unrounded). Different allophonic variants of a given phoneme will always share a number of phonetic features.

Let us sum up by repeating that the phoneme is the smallest contrastive unit (provisional definition); that its allophonic variants are phonetically similar; and that such variants exhibit either a free or a complementary distribution. To this must be added that every language has its own specific phonemic system that consists of a finite number of entities.

2.3. Distinctive features

Above, phonemes were defined negatively in that the definition of a given phoneme was that it was not any other phoneme. From this perspective English /d/, for example, can be characterized by not being /t/, /z/, /b/ or any other English phoneme. One method to describe a particular phoneme in a positive manner, is to specify those of its phonetic features which are especially important or linguistically significant. We can illustrate this by comparing /d/ to a number of other English consonants and extracting the articulatory features by which /d/ diverges from these consonants. A comparison of /d/ with /t/ will show that the vibrations of the vocal cords that normally accompany the pronunciation of /d/, are the distinguishing feature (/d/ is voiced, /t/ is voiceless). In relation to /z/ the articulation of /d/ is characterized by a complete blocking of the air-stream. If finally we compare /d/ to /b/, the place of articulation turns out to be of relevance seeing that /d/ has an alveolar place of articulation, while /b/ is a labial sound. These facts can be summarized thus:

/d/ ≠ /t/ voice/voicelessness
/d/ ≠ /z/ closure/friction
/d/ ≠ /b/ alveolar/labial

The features characteristic of /d/ are consequently: voice, closure and alveolar articulation, and we can therefore describe /d/ as a voiced, alveolar plosive. This is the combination of features by which the phoneme can be identified positively (and which is shared by no other phoneme). The features of a phoneme that are particularly relevant and which distinguish it from all other phonemes, are called *distinctive features*. Distinctive features can be described as commutable entities belonging to a lower level than phonemes, and we must therefore define them as the smallest contrastive linguistic units. This forces us to revise our provisional definition of phonemes, which we shall therefore characterize as 'the smallest, *purely successive* contrastive units'. Our revised definition emphasizes that, unlike distinctive features which may be simultaneous, phonemes always succeed one another in the spoken chain.

Much evidence can be adduced to show the important role that distinctive features play in language. Thus many linguistic rules can be expediently stated only in terms of distinctive features. A case in point is the regular formation of plurals in English. Phonemically, this rule consists in adding /-ɪz/ to words ending in /s, z, ʃ, ʒ, tʃ, dʒ/, /-s/ to words ending in /p, t, k, f, θ/ and /-z/ in all remaining cases, i.e. to words ending in final voiced consonants or in vowels. Since /s, z, ʃ, ʒ, tʃ, dʒ/ share the feature *sibilant* (they are all 'hissing' sounds) while /p, t, k, f, θ/ are all characterized by the feature *voicelessness* and the remaining phonemes by *voice*, the plural rule can be stated most exhaustively and most generally in the following manner (please note that the sibilant rule is to be applied first):

1. Plural → /-ɪz/ after (phonemes with the feature) sibilant (*horses*)
2.   -   → /-s/   -   - - -   voicelessness (*cats*)
3.   -   → /-z/   -   - - -   voice (*dogs*)

Such examples indicate that the resolution of a phoneme into distinctive features is not a mere phonetic description of how a phoneme manifests itself but also constitutes a division into components that are linguistically significant. It might be added that the conditions listed in item no. 3 of the rule could have been left out so that /-z/ is simply suffixed to words whose last segments do not have the features sibilant or voicelessness.

3. APPLIED PHONETICS

The preceding two chapters dealt with phonetics from a scientific point of view. But phonetics is not only of scientific interest; it also serves a practical purpose, which we shall now have a closer look at. Having discussed linguistic phonetics, we shall direct our attention to the application of phonetics in foreign-language teaching (applied phonetics).

For many years it has been a widely accepted view that the use of phonetics is a short cut to a good pronunciation of a foreign language. Instead of acquiring this through mere *imitation*, a more *analytic* and conscious approach can lead to better results. First, it is necessary to make a proper identification of the problems involved, and secondly, it is important to solve such problems in a deliberate manner.

To a large extent it is possible to predict the sort of pronunciation difficulties that a foreign learner will come across. Among other things, she can be expected to hear sounds that she has never heard before. She must learn not only to recognize and remember such sounds, but also to reproduce them herself. A Dane wanting to learn English will for instance be confronted with the sound [θ], which is non-existent in her own language. Having become able to recognize this sound when hearing it, she must try to learn how to produce it herself. The quickest way to do this is through detailed instruction as to how her organs of speech are to move; if she is told to place the tip of her tongue between her upper and lower teeth and blow while parting her lips, there is a good chance that she will rapidly acquire the right sound quality. It is thus possible for her to overcome her pronunciation difficulties by familiarizing herself with her organs of articulation, by consciously controlling them and by moving them in a specific way when producing a particular foreign sound. When she has learnt how to pronounce an unfamiliar sound, the next question will be when to use it and to know, for example, that /θ/ occurs in *thick* but not in *those*. The best methods to deal with such difficulties are to transcribe texts phonetically, to employ a pronouncing dictionary and, occasionally, to learn rules as to how certain written characters relate to pronunciation. Another predictable pronunciation problem is the fact that the intonation of a foreign language always diverges from that of the mother tongue. In this field, the best results will also be achieved if the foreign learner is informed of the characteristics of tonal patterns and how they differ from those of her native language, and if on a regular basis she attempts to produce typical and frequently occurring patterns of intonation. The few examples given above of problems to be anticipated and of how to solve them illustrate the usefulness of a deliberate approach to the teaching of the pronunciation of a foreign language. In his discussion of the advantages of such an analytic method, the American phonetician K.L. Pike (*Phonetics*, p. 20) says:

> ...a conscious, awkward, slow approach to a foreign language by conscious movements gains a closer approximation to native sounds and ultimately to a freer conversational style than can ever be attained (by an adult) by pure imitation.

For a foreign learner to acquire the pronunciation af a second language so well that she is taken for a native speaker, is of course a difficult task and one that takes many years. In most cases, she will have to accept less than ideal results. But what the foreign learner can do, is to improve her pronunciation to such a degree that she will always be fully understood by native speakers. For this purpose, it is pedagogically extremely useful to know the phonemes of the foreign language, for once the learner knows and masters the phonemes, she controls all linguistically relevant sound contrasts and will consequently be able to communicate freely. Conversely, if the learner does not learn the system of contrastive sound units, she must expect to be frequently misunderstood. Let us assume that a Danish learner has not yet learned the English phonemes /w/ and /z/. In words where these phonemes occur, she will replace them by the Danish sounds that bear the greatest resemblance to /w/ and /z/, i.e. /v/ and /s/. The implications of this are that she is unable to distinguish between minimal pairs such as *wine* ≠ *vine* and *zip* ≠ *sip*, and that, when she attempts to say *wine* and *zip*, she will be misunderstood by a native speaker, who will think that she said *vine* and *sip*. It is therefore immediately comprehensible that the minimum requirement for a learner who seeks always to make herself clearly understood in the foreign language, is that she knows and masters the phonemes of that language.

The replacement of English /w/ and /z/ by Danish /v/ and /s/ discussed above is an example of what is usually called *sound substitution*. The meaning of this term, then, is that the phonetically most similar sound in the mother tongue substitutes for a foreign sound. It is easy to understand that learners are inclined to interpret unknown sounds in terms of their own systemic sound patterns given the close ties between all human beings and their native language. Over a very long period of time we have grown accustomed to regarding only certain linguistic differences as linguistically relevant, and we have therefore difficulty in hearing and accepting new contrasts. Through intensive training we have also become virtuosos of mastering the sounds of the mother tongue, and the articulation has become so automatic that the production of all other sounds is rendered difficult.

One of the chief problems in learning the pronunciation of a foreign language is the learner's inclination to 'translate' the sounds of the foreign language into her own phonetic system. She will replace not only sounds that are completely unfamiliar to her but also those which resemble, but are not identical with, sounds in her own language. A Dane will, for instance, replace the 'dark' *l* in *shall* by Danish *l*, which is similar to, but not identical with, the English sound. This substitution is not likely to cause misunderstanding, but the native listener will find the pronunciation unusual. Another example is the inclination of Danes to replace the vowel in English *ball* by the corresponding, but not identical, vowel in Danish *måle*. English speakers will find this pronunciation peculiar as well, but it will hardly give rise to misunderstanding. Sound substitutions of this type explain at least in part why Danes speak English with 'a Danish accent'.

A learner who aims at acquiring a pronunciation which is both unequivocal and without a noticeable Danish accent, must try to grasp the difficulties associated with pronunciation errors deriving from Danish sound substitutions. In order to achieve this, it is not enough for the learner to acquire a thorough knowledge of English phonetics; she must also have some knowledge of Danish phonetics, so what is really required is a comparison between the phonetic systems of the two languages. Here the sound systems of English and Danish will be compared consistently, item by item. Such a survey will show that certain sounds are identical in the two languages, and in such cases no difficulties are likely to arise. There is, for instance, barely any difference between the two *n*-sounds in English *need* and Danish *nid*, and in English *mine* and Danish *meje* the two *m*-sounds correspond completely to each other. The two Danish nasals can consequently be used in English without the learner running the risk of sounding un-English or of being misunderstood. Wherever the sounds of the two languages are not identical, the learner must take great pains over her phonemes: first she should preferably do away with phonemic errors, and then she should try to remove all phonetic traces characteristic of a Danish accent. *Contrastive phonetics* is the only quick and safe way to predict potential pronunciation errors, and the learner will soon know the phonetic items on which she must concentrate and those which she can ignore. There is a need for contrastive phonetics: as we have seen, the native language interferes with the foreign language. We should perhaps add here that interference is by no means a phenomenon that is connected exclusively with phonetics; it is found also in the other components of language, and it is hardly too much to say that there is a need also for a *contrastive grammar*.

Let us repeat that there is general agreement that phonetics is a method by which the learner can take a short cut to the correct pronunciation of a foreign language, and hopefully we have now succeeded in convincing our readers of the plausibility of this assumption. While it is therefore fairly certain that a phonetic, analytic method is of avail for most of those who learn the pronunciation of a new language, it hardly needs saying that phonetic knowledge is of inestimable importance to those who teach the foreign language. If a language teacher does not have this knowledge but speaks the language well, she will probably be able to hear that something is wrong with the student's pronunciation and will, accordingly, be able to point out errors, but she will be in no position to define what is wrong or to prescribe how the errors should be remedied. Phonetic knowledge is thus a prerequisite for the successful teaching of pronunciation as is also argued in the following quotation by W.R. Lee (*In Honour of Daniel Jones*, pp. 291-292):

> Phonetic knowledge and ability are plainly essential to the teacher of English as a foreign language, whether or not English is his mother tongue, and this is widely though by no means universally acknowledged. It is one thing to hear something wrong with a pupil's pronunciation, another to put one's finger unerringly on the faults, another still to define those faults in terms of (say) movements of the speech-organs, and another again to invent remedial exercises when the pupil's imitation of the teacher fails, as it often does. Moreover, the teacher should himself be able to imitate accurately and pronounce the 'right' side by side with the 'wrong'. Possession of these skills presupposes a rigorous phonetic training, and this will include a study of phonetic theory as well as regular practical work, continuing for a year or more, to loosen the grip of mother-tongue listening and speaking habits.

Having established the central importance of phonetics to the teacher of pronunciation, we may finally ask how phonetics is best applied in teaching. A brief answer to this is that the teaching of pronunciation should be based on, rather than consist in, phonetics. A scholarly account of linguistic concepts such as phonemes, distinctive features, etc. is out of place in the classroom. Instead, the teacher should use her knowledge of the phonetic, rhythmic and tonal features of the language when required and not lose herself in theoretical deliberations. To a large extent, it is possible to avoid technical terminology by making use instead of expressions such as 'buzzing', 'clear' and 'dark'.

4. SOUND AND WRITING IN ENGLISH

There are various ways in which to represent speech in writing. In some languages the written characters reflect *morphemes* (e.g. in Chinese which has an ideogram for each morpheme), in others they reflect *syllables* (e.g. in Amharic), and in others still they represent *phonemes* (e.g. in European languages). We can therefore say that there are three different systems: morphemic (or ideographic) writing, syllabic writing and phonemic (or alphabetic) writing. In alphabetic writing, which unlike morphemic and syllabic writing presupposes a phonemic analysis, one letter corresponds to one phoneme – in principle at least, for there are many reasons why a one-to-one correspondence between letter and phoneme is never achieved in practice.

English exhibits a particularly high degree of inconsistency between sound and writing. In numerous cases one spelling represents two pronunciations, cf. *bow*, which can be pronounced /bəʊ/ ('a weapon for shooting arrows') as well as /baʊ/ ('bending of the head or body'), and *tear*, the spoken forms of which are /tɪə/ ('drop of water from the eye') and /teə/ ('pull to pieces'). Conversely, one pronunciation may reflect more than one spelling. Cases in point are /saɪt/, which may be spelled *sight*, *site* or *cite*, and /raɪt/, the orthographic representations of which are *right*, *rite*, *write* and *(wheel-)wright*. Words such as *though* (/ðəʊ/) and *victuals* (/vɪtlz/) clearly indicate that the English spelling system is by no means a consistently phonemic one.

There are several reasons for the gap between sound and writing in English. In the first place, English orthography reflects not Modern English pronunciation but rather Elizabethan speech. After Caxton had introduced the art of printing into England in 1476, an orthographic standardization was rapidly established, and English spelling has barely changed since then. Whereas writing thus came to a standstill centuries ago, pronunciation has changed radically from that time up to the present. Another reason for the discrepancy between sound and writing is that the letters of the English alphabet are outnumbered by the phonemes. There are only 26 letters to denote the 44 phonemes (normally) assigned to the English sound system, and the result of this is that not every phoneme can be represented uniliterally, i.e. be assigned one particular letter, and that therefore some must be expressed by means of a digraph (i.e. a combination of two letters). Instances of this are the phonemes /θ/, which is spelled with the digraph *th* (as in *think*), and /i:/, which has written counterparts such as *ea* and *ee* (*each*, *feel*). A more serious consequence of the restricted number of letters is the not infrequent failure to distinguish between phonemic differences in writing. There is thus no orthographic distinction between /s/ and /z/ in, for instance, *crisis* /kraɪsɪs/ and *bosom* /bʊzəm/, where both phonemes are denoted by *s*. In other words, difficulties arise because a job that requires 44 letters is performed by only 26.

The written form of English is thus not an adequate representation of the modern pronunciation; frequently it conceals significant differences of sound, and in addition it is often very irregular. A striking example of orthographic irregularity is the spelling *-ough*, which may be pronounced in no less than nine diffferent ways: *though* (/ðəʊ/), *through* (/θru:/), *cough* (/kɒf/), *plough* (/plaʊ/), *tough* (/tʌf/), *bought* (/bɔ:t/), *borough*

(/bʌrəl/), *hiccough* (/hɪkʌp/) and *hough* (/hɒk/). Obviously the foreign learner cannot, therefore, acquire a correct English pronunciation by taking spelling as his point of departure. On the contrary, he must rid himself of the misleading influence of orthography as quickly as possible and preferably before he has had a chance to memorize the written word, and before he assigns, as foreign learners are likely to, the sound values of the mother tongue to specific letters. With this end in view it is useful to read and write phonetic transcriptions which distinguish between all significant sound differences (which are the only distinctions to be indicated in a broad transcription). And it goes without saying that a maximum emphasis on oral proficiency will eventually remove orthographical interference.

In our discussion of English orthography so far, we have stressed the discrepancy between sound and writing, the frequent irregular spellings and the advisability of ignoring writing when attempting to acquire a correct pronunciation. But there is more to be said than that. Between 90 and 95 per cent of all English words have been shown to be spelled and pronounced according to regular patterns, and English spelling can therefore be regarded as predominantly regular. Irregular spelling, however, is to be found in frequently occurring words of English provenance (cf. words such as *does, any, many, women, blood*), the result being that as many as one fifth of all words represented on an average page of English literature exhibit irregular spelling. We must therefore reiterate that the beginner should not be introduced to English pronunciation via the written form of the language. Only when the learner has acquired the correct pronunciation of a not too narrow section of the English vocabulary, should he attempt to learn the rules and principles underlying the relationship between letters or combinations of letters and pronunciation.

We have just seen that English orthography is far from being arbitrary and by no means so inadequate as generally assumed. Nor do we immediately accept the objection often raised against the English writing system that it is not systematically phonemic and therefore not satisfactory. The orthographic systems of most other languages are not systematically phonemic either, and it is in fact questionable how useful a fully consistent phonemic writing system would be. If we were to stick to this principle, the vowels in the second syllables of the words *profane, profanity, profanation* would have to be spelled in three different ways (to denote the phonemes /eɪ/, /æ/ and /ə/). This would hardly be an expedient solution, for it would conceal that the three words share the morpheme *profan(e)* (i.e. that the words are cognate, being derived from each other). Also, the /eɪ/, /æ/, /ə/ alternation is an automatic one to native speakers and need therefore not be indicated graphically. The same alternation is to be found in a number of other words (e.g. *deprave, depravity, depravation; explain, explanatory, explanation*). If an Englishman were asked to pronounce the non-existent words **perclane, *perclanity, *perclanation*, he would have no hesitation in pronouncing them with, respectively, /eɪ/, /æ/ and /ə/. There can be little doubt that the best spelling system is not a strictly phonemic one but one that pays some attention to *morphological* relations and does not show phonemic variation which is predictable by a general rule. This is also the reason why the English plural morpheme is best denoted by the same letter although in some cases it reflects the phoneme /s/ (*cats*) and in others /z/ (*dogs*).

5. THE ENGLISH CONSONANTS

5.1. Vowels and consonants

The speech sounds of English and other languages can be assigned to two main categories, *vowels* and *consonants*, according to their *ability to form syllables and words*. We shall refrain from defining the English syllable because syllables are units that will be conceived as such intuitively both by speakers of English and of Danish. There will be no doubt in the minds of most Danes that for instance the following English words and compounds consist of, respectively, one, two, three and four syllables: *pay, paper, paper-weight, paper-money.*

Vowels are the speech sounds which, on their own, can function as syllables and, in some cases, also as (monosyllabic) words. Examples of the syllabic function of vowels are *appear* (/ə'pɪə/), *eternity* (/ɪ'tɜːnɪtɪ/) and *opaque* (/əʊ'peɪk/), the first syllables of which consist of vowels only (the last example having a diphthongal vowel). To illustrate that vowels can also function as words we may cite *are* (/ɑː/), *or, awe* (/ɔː/), *err* (/ɜː/), *ear* (/ɪə/), *I, eye* (/aɪ/), *air* (/eə/) and *owe* (/əʊ/). Consonants are speech sounds which in themselves can function neither as syllables nor as words (for the syllabic status of /l, m, n, ŋ/, see below). Typical examples of non-syllabic speech sounds in English are /p/, /t/, /f/, and /z/. Since every syllable consists of a vowel (or a diphthongal vowel) with or without consonants added, the syllable can be said to show unilateral dependence: consonants presuppose vowels, but vowels do not presuppose consonants. Vowels are therefore nuclear in the syllable, bearing syllabic function.

As there is always a vowel present in the syllable as we saw above, and since a vowel can be both preceded and followed by consonants, vowels can be said to take up the central position of the syllable. Conversely, the consonants dependent on them are placed marginally in the syllable. Two or more consonants often combine to fill this non-central position. /t/ or /s/ may, for example, be added to the final consonant in *park* (*parked, parks*), and if /s/ is added initially, the result will be *spark* (*sparked, sparks*). Words such as *strong* (/strɒŋ/) and *texts* (/teksts/) have, respectively, as many as three initial and four final consonants.

Some English speech sounds have both vocalic and consonantal features, being thereby difficult to classify. This holds true of /l/ and the nasals /m/, /n/ and /ŋ/. In *lull, maim, nine* and *sing* they are non-syllabic and therefore consonantal. But in words like *battle* (['bætl̩]), *open* (['əʊpm̩]), *redden* (['redn̩]) and *reckon* (['rekŋ̩]) they are syllabic and therefore vocalic. In the present book we regard these sounds as consonants, because the last group of examples may occasionally exhibit supporting vowels which take over the syllabic function. It should also be added that these syllabic consonants differ from the remaining stock of syllabic sounds (vowels) in that they never function as (independent) *words* or *accented* syllables.

Our classification of English speech sounds in two chief categories has been a *functional* one, and we shall now proceed to define the two categories *phonetically*.

Vowels are articulated with a relatively open speech tract, the air-stream being unobstructed and leaving the mouth along the centre; in auditory terms, vowels are sonorous sounds. The articulation of *consonants* is accompanied by a narrowing of the speech tract, which prevents the air-stream from escaping along the centre of the mouth. In the pronunciation of consonants like [p] and [d] the airflow is completely blocked, whereas for instance [z] and [ʃ] are produced with so much stricture as to cause audible friction. Finally, the air exhaled in the production of, for example, [m] and [l] escapes without being obstructed but not along the centre of the mouth: in the case of [m], it escapes through the nose and, in the case of [l], on one or both sides of the central narrowing.

5.2. The inventory of consonant phonemes

As discussed above in § 2.2, the phonemic inventory of a language can be established by finding pairs or whole series of words which are minimally different. A single list of words such as *pie, buy, tie, die, guy, fie, vie, thigh, thy, sigh, shy, high, my, nigh, lie, rye* and *why* supplies us with a stock of no less than 17 contrastive units: /p, b, t, d, g, f, v, θ, ð, s, ʃ, h, m, n, l, r, w/. A second series of words that are minimally different, *coo, chew, Jew, Zoo, you, pooh, boo, two, do, Sue, shoe, moo, loo, rue* and *woo*, adds another five consonants to our provisional inventory: /k, tʃ, dʒ, z, j/. By inserting different speech sounds in different phonetic sequences we have been able to show that initially there are 22 contrastive consonants, and this is in fact the total number in this position.

But consonants do not occur in initial position only, and it is therefore necessary to investigate contrastive occurrences in final position as well. The series *rip, rib, writ, rid, rich, ridge, rick* and *rig* reveals that /p, b, t, d, tʃ, dʒ, k, g/ have contrastive function also finally. An analysis of the series *pal, pam, pan* and *pang* shows us that this holds true also of /l/, /m/ and /n/, but there is an additional consonant phoneme /ŋ/ (the last segment of *pang*), which our investigation of consonants occurring initially in the syllable would not have uncovered. The three minimal pairs *life* ≠ *live* (adj.), *wreath* ≠ *wreathe* and *hiss* ≠ *his* prove that /f/ - /v/, /θ/ - /ð/ and /s/ - /z/ contrast also in final position, and the pair *ruche* ≠ *rouge* (/ru:ʃ/ ≠ /ru:ʒ/) reveals another new phoneme which like /ŋ/ never occurs initially. By adding the two new consonants /ŋ/ and /ʒ/ to the stock of units that occurred only initially, we get a total of 24, which is the final inventory of consonant phonemes. Further investigation into the lexicon of English will not enable us to add to this number. The following list illustrates the distribution of consonant phonemes in initial and final position:

/p/	/paɪ/	pie	/rɪp/	rip
/b/	/baɪ/	buy	/rɪb/	rib
/t/	/taɪ/	tie	/rɪt/	writ
/d/	/daɪ/	die	/rɪd/	rid
/tʃ/	/tʃu:/	chew	/rɪtʃ/	rich
/dʒ/	/dʒu:/	Jew	/rɪdʒ/	ridge

/k/	/kuː/	*coo*	/rɪk/	*rick*
/g/	/gaɪ/	*guy*	/rɪg/	*rig*
/f/	/faɪ/	*fie*	/laɪf/	*life*
/v/	/vaɪ/	*vie*	/laɪv/	*live* (adj.)
/θ/	/θaɪ/	*thigh*	/riːθ/	*wreath*
/ð/	/ðaɪ/	*thy*	/riːð/	*wreathe*
/s/	/saɪ/	*sigh*	/hɪs/	*hiss*
/z/	/zuː/	*Zoo*	/hɪz/	*his*
/ʃ/	/ʃaɪ/	*shy*	/ruːʃ/	*ruche*
/ʒ/			/ruːʒ/	*rouge*
/h/	/haɪ/	*high*		
/m/	/maɪ/	*my*	/pæm/	*pam*
/n/	/naɪ/	*nigh*	/pæn/	*pan*
/ŋ/			/pæŋ/	*pang*
/l/	/laɪ/	*lie*	/pæl/	*pal*
/r/	/raɪ/	*rye*		
/w/	/waɪ/	*why*		
/j/	/juː/	*you*		

The empty slots in this table should be noted. Apart from the non-presence of two entities (/ŋ/ and /ʒ/) in initial position, there are four consonants that never occur in final position (/h, r, w, j/) and which would have remained hidden if the commutation test had been restricted to this position. Out of the 24 consonant phonemes of English, six are clearly of restricted occurrence.

5.3. The system of consonants

After establishing the English consonantal inventory, our next step is a *classification* of the units represented and an investigation of their *systemic* interrelations.

In accordance with their *manner of articulation* English consonants can be assigned to two general categories: *obstruents* and *sonorants*. The production of obstruents entails a narrowing of the speech channel so that the airflow is prevented from escaping freely. In the articulation of sonorants, which are produced with greater sonority than obstruents, there is no obstruction to impede the escape of air. Obstruents can be subdivided into *stops* (/p, t, tʃ, k, b, d, dʒ, g/) and *fricatives* (/f, v, θ, ð, s, z, ʃ, ʒ, h/). Stops can be either *affricated* (/tʃ, dʒ/) or *unaffricated* (/p, t, k, b, d, g/); the latter are also called *plosives*. An affricated stop (or an *affricate*) has a release stage which is performed so slowly that friction arises at the place of articulation in the oral cavity. The slow release stage is what distinguishes an affricate from an unaffricated stop (plosive). Like the stops, fricatives have two subclasses: *sibilants* (/s, z, ʃ, ʒ/) and *non-sibilants* (/f, v, θ, ð, h/). Sibilants are referred to as such because of the hissing friction that is produced when the air-stream escapes through a narrow groove along the centre of the tongue. Because of the shape of the tongue sibilants are also called '*groove-type*' fricatives. In the articulation of non-sibilants no hissing sound is produced: the opening from side to side between the flat tongue and the palate is formed like a slit. Non-sibilants may therefore also be denoted as '*slit-type*' fricatives. English sonorants may be classified in three subdivisions: *nasals* (/m, n, ŋ/), *semi-vowels* (/w, j/) and *liquids* (/l, r/). The defining characteristic of the articulation of a nasal is a lowering of the soft palate so that the resonance of the nasal cavity is added. Semi-vowels allow the airflow to escape through the centre of the mouth, thereby showing phonetic resemblance to the vowels (however, specimens such as *twin* and *cute* /kju:t/ exhibit narrowing and audible friction). Liquids, which are characterized by a raising of the tongue towards the palate in the centre of the mouth, can be subdivided into *laterals* (/l/) and *non-laterals* (/r/). Laterals exhibit contact between tongue and palate, forcing the air to escape on one or both sides of the tongue. Our division of English consonants into categories and subcategories according to manner of articulation may be summarized by means of the following diagram:

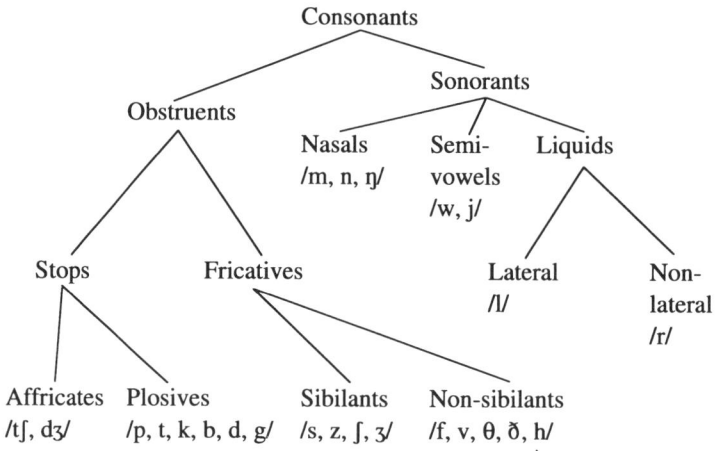

As far as *place of articulation* is concerned, English consonants fall into eight groups: *bilabial* (/p, b, m, w/), *labiodental* (/f, v/), *dental* (/θ, ð/), *alveolar* (/t, d, s, z, n, l, r/), *palato-alveolar* (/tʃ, dʒ, ʃ, ʒ/), *palatal* (/j/), *velar* (/k, g, ŋ/) and *glottal* (/h/). Only the term labiodental, which indicates displaced articulation, includes the active articulator for labelling the area of articulation. The remaining terms each imply that the active articulator lies immediately opposite or very close to the passive articulator. It might be added that, with the exception of /h/, all English consonants have their places of articulation where the greatest degree of narrowing occurs in the oral cavity. Since /h/ is produced with an open oral passage, the glottis is best seen as its place of articulation.

In terms of *phonation*, the consonants can finally be classified in two categories: *voiceless* (/p, t, tʃ, k, f, θ, s, ʃ, h/) and *voiced* (/b, d, dʒ, g, v, ð, z, ʒ, m, n, ŋ, w, j, l, r/). Apart from /h/, all voiceless consonants have exact voiced counterparts in terms of place and manner of articulation: /θ/, for instance, is the voiceless equivalent of /ð/. It should be noted that the system of obstruents has a consistent contrast of voice applicable to all members except for /h/. All sonorants, on the other hand, are voiced, phonation having therefore no distinctive function in the sonorant system.

On the basis of the three criteria of classification just discussed we may now draw up the English system of consonants. In the table below, our classification according to manner of articulation is not complete in that the subdivision of stops and fricatives has been left out. But the categorization of place of articulation into eight areas has been retained:

			Bilabial	Labiodental	Dental	Alveolar	Palato-alveolar	Palatal	Velar	Glottal
Obstruents	Stops	voiceless	p			t	tʃ		k	
		voiced	b			d	dʒ		g	
	Fricatives	voiceless		f	θ	s	ʃ			h
		voiced		v	ð	z	ʒ			
Sonorants	Nasals		m			n			ŋ	
	Semi-vowels		w					j		
	Lateral liquids					l				
	Non-lateral liquids					r				

(Manner of articulation / Place of articulation)

In this system each consonant is distinguished from the rest. We are now able to describe English /v/ as a voiced, labiodental fricative, /tʃ/ as a voiceless, palato-alveolar (affricated) stop, /ŋ/ as a velar nasal, /j/ as a palatal semi-vowel, /r/ as a(n) (alveolar) non-lateral liquid, etc. Since /w/ also has raising of the back of the tongue in the direction of the velum, it will later (§ 5.13) be classified as a labial-velar semi-vowel.

5.4. Comparison with Danish

Having thus established the consonant phonemes of English and described their systemic interrelations, we shall return to what we said in Chapter 3 concerning the usefulness of comparing English and Danish item by item. Such a comparison will uncover the differences between the two languages and enable us to identify the difficulties of pronunciation that the Danish learner will come across.

The consonants of Standard Danish are /p, t, k, b, d, g, f, s, ʃ, h, v, ð, m, n, ŋ, l, r, j/ as exemplified by the following series of words: *pande, tænde, kande, bande, danne, genne, finde, sande, sjæle, Hanne, vande, bade* (/ˈbaːðə/), *mande, nænne, synge* (/ˈsøŋə/), *lande, rande* and *jolle*. The 18 Danish units may be compared to the 24 English consonants by means of the two diagrams given below:

	English					Danish		
p	t	tʃ	k		p	t		k
b	d	dʒ	g		b	d		g
f	θ	s	ʃ	h	f		s	ʃ	h
v	ð	z	ʒ		v	ð		r
w	l r	j				l	j	
m	n	ŋ			m	n	ŋ	

English consonants without Danish equivalents are framed by solid lines. The reverse, Danish consonants having no counterparts in English, does not apply with the possible exception of /r/. The broken lines of the diagrams signify our difficulty in determining whether this is a case of equivalence. Even if English /r/ and Danish /r/ are spelled by means of the same letter, they diverge in both place and manner of articulation, the English sound being an alveolar, non-lateral liquid and the Danish sound being a uvular-pharyngeal fricative. The diagrams show that six English units (/tʃ, dʒ, ʒ, z, θ, w/) have no Danish counterparts. We may predict that Danes will have difficulty in perceiving as well as rendering these consonants, and that Danes will be likely to replace them by the systemic units of their own language that bear the greatest resemblance to the English consonants. In the English word *thigh* Danes will thus tend to replace /θ/ by /s/ (*sigh*). Being phonemic errors, such sound substitutions will have semantic consequences, and they must therefore be corrected without delay. This requires exercises that consist in identifying word pairs such as *thigh-sigh, wail-veil, zip-sip*, etc., where the unfamiliar consonants are confronted with the well-known and systemically closest units.

When the Danish learner has surmounted his difficulties in pronouncing /tʃ, dʒ, ʒ, z, θ, w/ correctly, he will probably be able to pronounce all English consonants unequivocally. But a number of phonetic problems remain to be dealt with. It is true that consonantal sounds such as [v], [ð] and [l] occur in both languages, but their pronunciations differ somewhat, and if the Danish learner substitutes his native sounds for the English ones, they will be perceived by the English speaker as indications of an unfamiliar and strange accent. If for instance the Danish learner uses his native [ð]-sound, which unlike the English consonant is very lax, he may well not be fully understood and will be identified as a foreigner. He should therefore practise the correct pronunciation also of these consonants.

In addition to the problems discussed above, difficulties arise in pronouncing well-known sounds in unfamiliar combinations or in unfamiliar positions in syllables or words. An Englishman trying to learn Danish has difficulty in combining familiar sounds such as /g/, /k/, and /n/ in the clusters /gn-/ and /kn-/ in, e.g., the Danish words *gnaske* and *knække* (conversely, Danes will have little difficulty in leaving out these sequences when speaking English). Another imbalance between the two languages concerns the plosives. Whereas in English /p, t, k/ and /b, d, g/ occur in initial, final and medial positions, having contrastive functions in all three places, these phonemes show a more restricted occurrence and less distinctive power in Danish. Accordingly, Danes have problems with pronouncing the familiar sounds [p], [t] and [k] in words such as *supper, better* and *liquor* and in distinguishing between words like *bigger* and *bicker*. (For more details, see below, § 5.7.)

5.5. The release stage of stops

In words such as *supper, ebbing, settee, redeem, marching, ledger, knocking*, and *vigour*, the articulation of /p, b, t, d, tʃ, dʒ, k, g/ comprises three stages: the *closing, compression* and *release* stages. The speech channel is open in the articulation of both [ʌ] and [ə] in, e.g., *supper*. The first stage of [p] consists here in a closing of the lips, the second stage is one in which the exhalation air is compressed behind the bilabial closure, and in the third stage the air escapes with audible noise (explosion) when the lips part. The second stage is the only one of the three always to be present, and in affricates the third stage is present as well. But the remaining stages may be left out as for example when an initial plosive (as in *blimey*) is pronounced after a pause during which the mouth has been closed. And in a question like *Is it ripe?* in which [p] immediately precedes a pause, the third stage may be omitted if the final bilabial closure is retained.

Of the three articulatory stages of the stops the release stage is the most noteworthy because of the abrupt escape of compressed air. Below we shall discuss the various ways in which this stage may be brought about:

(1) *Affrication.* – The palato-alveolar stops /tʃ/ and /dʒ/ are released so slowly that a fricative element ([ʃ] and [ʒ]) arises in the same area of articulation as that in which the closure is made. In other words, the tip and blade of the tongue is lowered so slowly from the palate that friction is heard as the compressed air escapes after the release. In the diagram below the converging lines to the left illustrate how the two articulators move together. The line above the figure '2' shows how the articulators form a hold together, and the diverging lines to the right indicate how they again part, first slowly, then more rapidly:

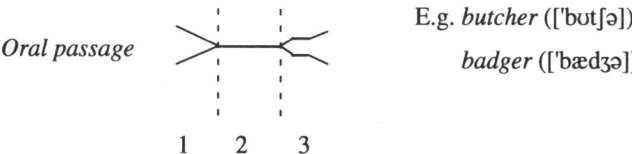

(2) *Nasal release.* – When plosives are followed by homorganic nasals (i.e. nasals articulated by means of the same organs at the same place), the release of air takes place not in the mouth as it usually does but through the nose by a lowering of the velum. The two diagrams below illustrate the positions of the oral and nasal passages during the three stages of plosives with, respectively, oral and nasal release:

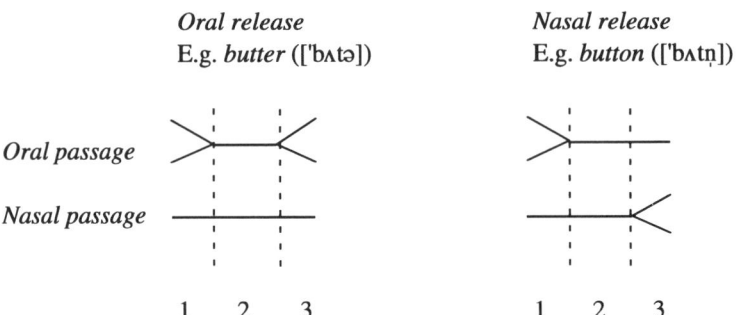

In both *butter* and *button* the first stage in the articulation of [t] leads to a closure in which both the oral and nasal passages are blocked. In the third stage – and this is where the two [t]s differ – the release of [t] in *butter* is effected by a reopening of the oral passage whereas in *button* the release is brought about by opening the nasal valve.

As examples of bilabial plosives followed by a nasal we may cite *open* [ˈəʊpm̩] and *rip (th)em* [ˈrɪpm̩]. In the case of the velar plosives /k/ and /g/, nasal release is not very common, but may occasionally occur in rapid speech in words like *bacon* and *organ*, pronounced [ˈbeɪkŋ̍] and [ˈɔːgŋ̍] instead of [ˈbeɪkən] and [ˈɔːgən].

(3) *Lateral release.* – When the alveolar plosives /t/ and /d/ are followed by the homorganic lateral phoneme /l/, the tip of the tongue remains in contact with the alveolar ridge, the release taking place laterally, i.e. not, as is normal, through the centre of the mouth but on one or both sides of the tongue. Instances of this type of release are *cattle* [ˈkætl̩] and *middle* [ˈmɪdl̩]. We may consequently distinguish between two kinds of oral release: central release (as in *batter*) and lateral release (as in *battle*).

(4) *Aspiration.* – In their third stage the voiceless plosives /p, t, k/ are usually modified by aspiration. The glottis remains open for a short while after the release of the plosives in, e.g., *pea*, *tea* and *key*, a short voiceless *h*-like interval arising in which the air is expelled before the articulation of the following vowel is initiated: [pʰiː, tʰiː, kʰiː]. The duration of this interval varies, being occasionally omitted. In accented, initial position (e.g. *pin*, *team*, *cold*) the aspiration of plosives is relatively long. In unaccented position (e.g. *police*, *letter*) and finally (e.g. *lip*, *hat*) the aspiration is considerably shorter, and after initial /s/ it is non-existent (e.g. *spin*, *steam*, *scold*); this means that in the last case the vocal cords begin to vibrate immediately the closure is released. Our two next diagrams show the coordination between oral and glottal activity in the articulation of aspirated and unaspirated plosives: the straight lines at the bottom represent voicelessness (open glottis), and the wavy lines signify voice (vibrating vocal cords):

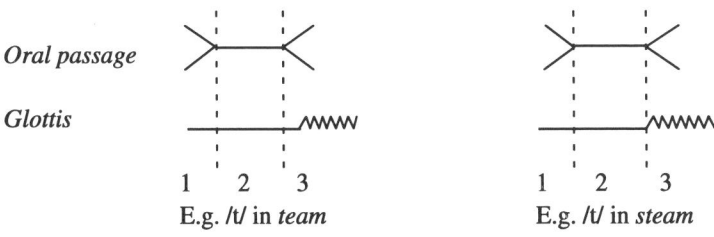

5.6. The distinction between voiced and voiceless stops

Above in § 5.3, English consonants were divided into two groups on the basis of phonation, those of one group being voiced and those of the other, voiceless. The two categories of stops thus arising can be classified in four pairs distinguished by voice contrasts: /p/ - /b/, /t/ - /d/, /tʃ/ - /dʒ/ and /k/ - /g/. We shall now subject the distinctions between the two categories of stops to a closer examination. For even if they are called voiceless and voiced, absence and presence of voice are certainly not the only properties by which the two categories are distinguished. If we make the experiment of whispering the word pairs *peak-beak*, *two-do*, *char-jar* and *come-gum*, the vocal cords no longer vibrate. Since the difference between each of the two components of the pairs is clearly retained, other features than voice must be present to signal the distinction. As it turns out, voice is only one among the following phonetic properties that enable us to distinguish between /p, t, tʃ, k/ and /b, d, dʒ, g/:

(1) *Aspiration*. – Whereas /b, d, g/ exhibit no aspiration, /p, t, k/ are normally aspirated. As mentioned above in § 5.5, the aspiration is especially strong in accented, initial position.

(2) *Force of articulation*. – The stops /p, t, tʃ, k/ are produced with greater force than /b, d, dʒ, g/. The additional expenditure of energy shows itself in, among other things, a longer duration of the compression stage, a stronger expulsion of breath in the release stage and greater muscular tension.

(3) *Voicing*. – /p, t, tʃ, k/ are always voiceless, but /b, d, dʒ, g/ are often accompanied by voice. In medial position when occurring between voiced sounds, /b, d, dʒ, g/ (in e.g. *neighbour*, *shudder*, *ledger* and *hugging*) are fully voiced. In other positions, however, voicing turns out to be a less stable feature. In final position, for instance in *tube*, *lead*, *ridge* and *league*, they are either weakly voiced with vocal-cord vibration only at the beginning or – and this is more frequent – completely voiceless. Initial /b, d, g/ may be realised with weak vocal-cord vibration setting in towards the end of the second stage, or they may be pronounced without any voice at all. The affricate /dʒ/ when occurring initially is most often voiced during its last part, i.e. in its release stage.

(4) *Length of preceding sounds*. – When /p, t, tʃ, k/ occur finally in the syllable, the length of a preceding vowel (or nasal or lateral) is considerably reduced. Accordingly, the vowels of *hop*, *heat*, *rich* and *leak* are relatively short, whereas in e.g. *hob*, *heed*, *ridge* and *league* full vowel length is retained before final /b, d, dʒ, g/. In medial

position the length of vowels is also reduced; in, e.g., *writer* and *litre* the accented vowels are somewhat shorter than in *rider* and *leader*.

By means of the above four features we are able to distinguish /p, t, tʃ, k/ and /b, d, dʒ, g/. Force of articulation always differentiates the two classes,[1] the relative contribution of the remaining features as contrastive indicators being dependent on position in syllable and word according to the following pattern:

Initially in accented syllable. – The plosives /p, t, k/ are aspirated and voiceless, while /b, d, g/ are unaspirated and partially voiced or voiceless. The stable – and therefore decisive – feature in this position is aspiration. The affricates /tʃ/ and /dʒ/ differ in terms of voice and force of articulation in initial position. The following words illustrate these contrasts:

pin	*tin*	*chin*	*cod*
bin	*din*	*gin*	*god*

Medially, preceding unaccented syllable. – In this position /p, t, tʃ, k/ are voiceless, they reduce the length of preceding sounds, and (with the exception of /tʃ/) they are weakly aspirated. /b, d, dʒ, g/, on the other hand, are fully voiced and unaspirated, and they do not reduce the length of preceding sounds. These features in combination distinguish the two series. We may exemplify the medial contrasts by means of the following words:

rapid	*latter*	*riches*	*bicker*
rabid	*ladder*	*ridges*	*bigger*

Finally. – Final /p, t, tʃ, k/ are voiceless, reducing the length of preceding vowels (or nasals or laterals) perceptibly. If released, /p, t, k/ are also weakly aspirated. /b, d, dʒ, g/ are weakly voiced or voiceless and unaspirated, having no reductive effect on preceding sounds. In this position the length of a preceding vowel (or nasal or lateral) is the decisive factor. The following examples may be cited:

hop	*cat*	*rich*	*leak*
hob	*cad*	*ridge*	*league*

We have just seen that /p, t, tʃ, k/ and /b, d, dʒ, g/ are distinguished in both initial, medial and final positions. But they are not always contrasted. After initial /s/ e.g. *spin*, *steam*, *scold* the plosives /p, t, k/ and /b, d, g/ are never opposed; that is to say that no English word pairs distinguish initial /sp-, st-, sk-/ from /sb-, sd-, sg-/. The words cited may therefore be interpreted in two ways: either as /spɪn, stiːm, skəʊld/ or as /sbɪn, sdiːm, sgəʊld/ as if phonemically they contain either /p, t, k/ or /b, d, g/. In phonetics the suspension of a phonemic contrast is called *neutralisation*. Here the

---

1. For this reason many phoneticians prefer the labels *fortis* (strong) and *lenis* (weak) about the two groups of consonants traditionally referred to as voiceless and voiced.

distinction between English /p, t, k/ and /b, d, g/ has been neutralised in post-initial position, i.e. initially after /s/. In the present book such plosives will be regarded as realisations of /p, t, k/.

5.7. A comparison between English and Danish stops

English has two stops, the affricates /tʃ/ and /dʒ/, which have no equivalents in Danish, and which will therefore create problems for the Danish learner. We will discuss this in our treatment of the individual stops.

Danish /p, t, k/ are realised with strong aspiration, whereas /b, d, g/ are unaspirated. This is the only genuine difference between the two classes, which are both voiceless and relatively weakly articulated. Since the distinction in English between initial /p, t, k/ and /b, d, g/ is effected by means of aspiration as mentioned above in § 5.6, voice and force of articulation being less important, the Danish learner may transfer his Danish plosives to English without any risk of being misunderstood or sounding un-English. The plosives of Danish *pil-bil, tælle-delle* and *kilde-gilde* may consequently be used for the pronunciation of English *pill-bill, tell-dell* and *kill-gill*.

But unlike Danish, English contrasts all stops both medially and finally, distinguishing numerous word pairs with /p, t, tʃ, k/ and /b, d, dʒ, g/, cf. *writer ≠ rider, tripe ≠ tribe*, etc. In Danish words, /p, t, k/ and /b, d, g/ are only distinguished initially (cf. *pil ≠ bil, tag ≠ dag, kår ≠ går*) and medially before accented vowels (cf. *kapere ≠ barbere, partere ≠ gardere, lakere ≠ agere*) or before unaccented, but qualitatively full vowels (cf. *Ota ≠ Oda, manko ≠ mango*). In all other positions the contrasts between Danish /p, t, k/ and /b, d, g/ have been neutralised. Medially before vowels that are both unaccented and qualitatively reduced, the pronunciation is always [b, d, g]. Words such as *lappe* and *lækker* are pronounced in precisely the same way as *labbe* and *lægger* with, respectively, [b] and [g]. In word-final position only [b, d, g] occur in non-final words in utterances (i.e., the labial plosive that is present in, e.g., the phrase *en kop i hånden* is a [b]), and in final words of utterances there is free variation between [p, t, k] and [b, d, g] (i.e., the last word in an utterance such as *ræk mig den hat* is sometimes pronounced with aspiration ([hat]) and sometimes without ([had]). And as a final point, the distinction between /p, t, k/ and /b, d, g/ is neutralised post-initially after /s/ just as in English (e.g. in *sparke, stol, skole*).

Danes have become so accustomed to neutralising plosives medially (before unaccented and reduced vowels) and finally that they will automatically transfer their neutralisations to English. They will therefore have difficulty in hearing any difference between English word pairs such as *latter-ladder* and *cap-cab*. And in producing these words, they will tend to pronounce both *latter* and *ladder* as ['lædə] and to render both *cab* and *cap* indiscriminately as [kæp] and [kæb]. In order to avoid such errors, the Danish learner will be well advised to train himself in identifying the word pairs listed below and in producing them correctly by voicing [b, d, g] fully and aspirating [p, t, k] slightly in medial position, and by considerably reducing the length of sounds preceding /p, t, k/ in final position:

Medial		Final	
voiceless, asp.	voiced, unasp.	short vowel	long vowel
rapid	*rabid*	*tripe*	*tribe*
Epping	*ebbing*	*rope*	*robe*
simple	*symbol*	*rip*	*rib*
latter	*ladder*	*hat*	*had*
matter	*madder*	*wrote*	*road*
eaten	*Eden*	*joint*	*joined*
bicker	*bigger*	*tack*	*tag*
vicar	*vigour*	*dock*	*dog*
ankle	*angle*	*leak*	*league*

It is to be expected that the contrast between /tʃ/ and /dʒ/ will cause problems for the Danish learner in these positions even after the correct pronunciation has been acquired initially, and it is therefore advisable that he trains himself also in this distinction:

Medial		Final	
voiceless	voiced	short	long
batches	*badges*	*etch*	*edge*
riches	*ridges*	*beseech*	*besiege*
catcher	*cadger*	*larch*	*large*

5.8. The stop phonemes

Below, the English consonants will be described individually. In each case four items will be taken into account:

1. A description of the *articulation* of the consonant.
2. A discussion of the most important *allophonic variants* of the consonantal phoneme in question.
3. A comparison with related consonants in *Danish*; whenever needed, word lists, etc. will be provided for exercise purposes.
4. An account of *spellings* with special emphasis on the regular correspondences between sound and writing.

Reference to previous sections will be given to the extent that they deal with the four items.

/p/

(1) *Articulation.* – In the pronunciation of this voiceless, bilabial plosive the glottis is open and the velum raised. Moving upwards, the lower lip forms a closure with the upper lip. The airflow is interrupted, air being compressed behind the place of articulation until the lip closure is released.

(2) *Variation.* – The amount of aspiration varies as described in § 5.5 and § 5.6. See also § 5.5 for /p/ with nasal release.

(3) *Comparison with Danish.* – See § 5.7.

(4) *Spellings.* – /p/ is spelled with *p* and *pp*, cf. *pop, supper.* In *pneumonia, pseudo, psychology, receipt, cupboard* there is no [p].

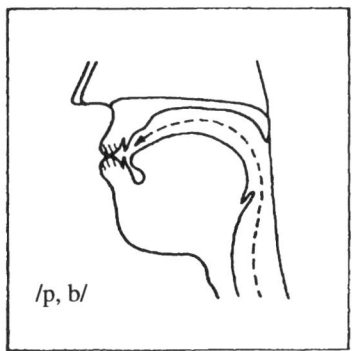

/p, b/

/b/

(1) *Articulation.* – /b/ is a voiced, bilabial plosive. The setting of the organs of speech is identical with that of /p/ except that the vocal cords may vibrate.

(2) *Variation.* – The amount of voice varies as described in § 5.6. See § 5.5 for /b/ with nasal release.

(3) *Comparison with Danish.* – Danish /b/ is always voiceless unlike English /b/, which is frequently accompanied by voice. Cf. also § 5.7.

(4) *Spellings.* – /b/ is spelled with *b* and *bb*, cf. *ball, ribbon.* In *lamb, thumb, debt* and *doubt* there is no [b].

/t/

(1) *Articulation.* – In the pronunciation of this voiceless, alveolar plosive, the glottis is open and the velum raised. Moving upwards, the tip of the tongue forms a closure with the alveolar ridge. The air-stream is interrupted, a compression of air building up behind the alveolar closure until it is released. The lips are parted.

(2) *Variation.* – The amount of aspiration varies as described in § 5.5 and § 5.6. See also § 5.5 for /t/ with nasal and lateral release.

(3) *Comparison with Danish.* – Some Copenhagen accents exhibit a strongly affricated plosive [ts], which should not be transferred to English. Cf. also § 5.7.

(4) *Spellings.* – /t/ is spelled with *t* and *tt* in *motel, attune*. In a few words *th* represents /t/, cf. *Thames, Thomas, thyme*. In *ballet, bouquet, cabaret, christen, listen, hasten* there is no [t].

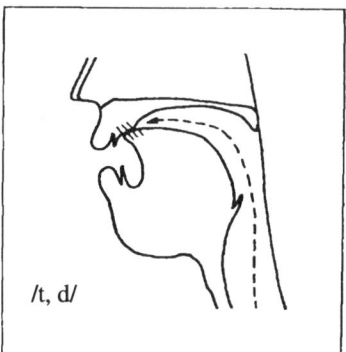

/d/

(1) *Articulation.* – /d/ is a voiced, alveolar plosive. The setting of the organs of speech is identical with that of /t/ except that the vocal cords may vibrate.

(2) *Variation.* – The amount of voice varies as described in § 5.6. See § 5.5 for /d/ with nasal and lateral release.

(3) *Comparison with Danish.* – Danish /d/ is always voiceless unlike English /d/, which is often voiced. Cf. also § 5.7.

(4) *Spellings.* – /d/ is spelled with *d* and *dd* as in *dope, addict*. In *handkerchief* and *handsome* there is no [d].

/tʃ/

(1) *Articulation.* – This voiceless, palato-alveolar affricate is produced with an open glottis and a raised velum. The tip, blade and front of the tongue are raised, forming a closure with the alveolar ridge and front part of the hard palate. The airflow being interrupted, the air is compressed behind the place of articulation. When the closure is released, the tongue is lowered so slowly from the palate that friction occurs between the alveolar ridge and hard palate on the one hand and the blade and front of the tongue on the other. In the release stage the tongue is grooved as in the pronunciation of [ʃ] or [ʒ]. The lips are parted and rounded.

(2) *Variation.* – There are no important allophonic variants of this phoneme.

(3) *Comparison with Danish.* – The consonantal system of Danish having no voiceless, palato-alveolar stop, Danes tend to replace the initial consonant in English words such as *charge* and *chimney* by a related consonant cluster from Danish, /tj/, which occurs in Danish *tjene, tjære, tjavs*, etc. This combination of consonants is normally realised as [t] + devoiced [j], but [tʃ] is also a possible realisation. Danish can therefore be said to have free variation between [tj] and [tʃ]. That is not the case in English. Young educated English speakers commonly realise /tj/ as /tʃ/ but not the other way round, and most educated speakers still distinguish carefully between the two pronunciations: in a word like *cheap* the pronunciation is, of course, [tʃ], *ch* being the orthographic rendering of the phoneme /tʃ/; in, e.g., *tube* [tj] is the only pronunciation possible for these speakers, *t(u)* representing the phonemic sequence /tj/. As foreign learners Danes should stick to the most general (non-advanced) forms and are therefore well advised to maintain the distinction. They should train themselves in distinguishing between /tʃ/ in e.g., *chew, choosy, cherry, choke* and /tj/ in, e.g., *tutor, Tuesday, tune, tutelage*. The correct pronunciation of [tʃ] may be acquired in the following way: start out by saying [ʃ] as described below in § 5.10 and interrupt this sizzling sound by raising the tip of the tongue to a [t] closure (Danes often use this combined sound – *sht!* – for shushing people). Then the learner should once again say [ʃ] by releasing the closure and retract the tip of the tongue, at the same time rounding and pushing forward his lips. In pronouncing, e.g., the word *choose* with its initial combined sound, he should aim at making the friction noise strong and deep. After mastering the sound in isolation and in individual words, the learner may find it useful to have a go at the following tongue-twisters:

The charlady was enchanted by the rich butcher from Chingford.
Three charming children fetched the chairs from the porch.
Satchmo's concerto in Chile was wretched.
Mitchell's cherubic children were watching the chase cheerfully.
Charles was checkmated and didn't have much choice.

(4) *Spellings.* – /tʃ/ is spelled with *ch* and *tch*, cf. *child, patch.* *ti* and *t(u)* may render /tʃ/ in medial position, cf. *question, culture.*

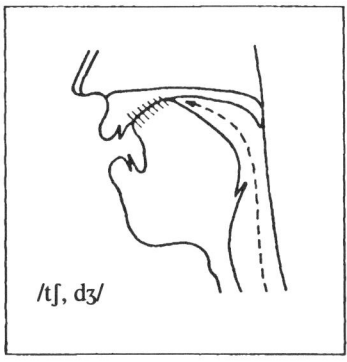

/dʒ/

(1) *Articulation.* – /dʒ/ is a voiced, palato-alveolar affricate. The setting of the organs of speech is identical with that of /tʃ/ except that the vocal cords may vibrate.

(2) *Variation.* – The amount of voice varies as described in § 5.6.

(3) *Comparison with Danish.* – The Danish consonantal system having no voiced, palato-alveolar stop, Danes can be expected to replace the initial consonant of English words such as *jackal* and *giraffe* by a phonetically related consonant cluster, /dj/, which occurs initially in Danish *djærv*, *djævel* and *Djursland*, etc. This represents a phonemic error, which may lead to misunderstanding. It is true that in the speech of many young educated English speakers /dʒ/ and /dj/ are both realised as /dʒ/ (cf. above concerning /tj/ realised as /tʃ/), but if /dʒ/ in *jewel* is replaced by /dj/, the word will be conceived as *duel*. It will therefore be useful for the Danish learner to train himself in the perception and pronunciation of word pairs such as:

/dʒ/	/d/ + /j/
Jew	*dew*
juke-box	*duke*
Julie	*duly*
June	*dune*
juice	*deuce*

The correct pronunciation of [dʒ] may be acquired in the same way as [tʃ], but the sound must be voiced, its articulation being somewhat weaker. After mastering the pronunciation of, e.g., *char*, *chin* and *riches*, the learner may proceed to pronounce *jar*, *gin* and *ridges*, adding vocal-cord vibration and with reduced force of articulation. Having mastered the sound in isolation and in individual words, the learner may practise longer sequences such as:

> *The giant wore a large suit of pyjamas.*
> *Nigel joined Jack near the junction.*
> *We were obliged to play bridge with the surgeon and his huge wife.*
> *George jumped up and barged into the juggler.*
> *The judge addressed the jury jubilantly.*

(4) *Spellings.* – /dʒ/ is spelled with *j* as in *jelly*, *jaw* and with *g* in front of *e*, *i*, *y* as in *page*, *ginger*, *gyp*. *d(u)* and *d(i)* may render /dʒ/ in medial position, cf. *verdure*, *soldier*.

/k/

(1) *Articulation.* – In the pronunciation of this voiceless, velar plosive the glottis is open and the velum raised. The back of the tongue is raised, forming a closure with the velum so that the airflow is interrupted. A compression of air builds up behind the place of articulation until the velar closure is released. The lips are parted.

(2) *Variation.* – The amount of aspiration varies as described in § 5.5 and § 5.6. See also § 5.5 concerning /k/ with nasal release. The precise place of articulation of /k/ depends on the quality of adjacent vowels, cf. § 2.2.

(3) *Comparison with Danish.* – See § 5.7.

(4) *Spellings.* – /k/ is spelled with *k* (*king, lurk*), *ck*, (*pick, beckon*) and with *c* when followed by a consonant or by one of the written vowels *a, o, u* or when in final position (*climb, callous, cost, curate, logic*). In for example *knee, knit* and *know* there is no [k].

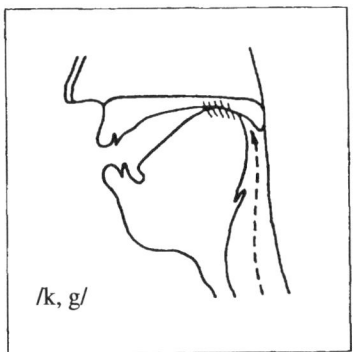

/k, g/

/g/

(1) *Articulation.* – /g/ is a voiced, velar plosive. The setting of the organs of speech is identical with that of /k/ except that the vocal cords may vibrate.

(2) *Variation.* – The amount of voice varies as described in § 5.6. See § 5.5 for /g/ with nasal release. The precise place of articulation of /g/ depends on the quality of adjacent vowels: it is palatal before front vowels (*geese*) and velar before central and back vowels (*girl, got*).

(3) *Comparison with Danish.* – Danish /g/ is always voiceless unlike English /g/, which is frequently voiced. Cf. also § 5.7.

(4) *Spellings.* – /g/ is spelled with *g* when followed by a consonant or by one of the written vowels *a, o, u* or when in final position (*glad, gasoline, gospel, gull, rag*). In for example *gnash, gnat* and *sign, paradigm* there is no [g].

The glottal plosive [ʔ]

In addition to the eight stops discussed above English has a *glottal plosive*, which is denoted by the symbol [ʔ]. Being primarily a phonetic entity, this sound has not normally any contrastive linguistic function and consequently is not included in the phonemic inventory of English.

In the articulation of [ʔ] the glottis is closed completely so that the passage of air is interrupted. Air pressure builds up below the glottis, but the closure is quickly released by the sudden separation of the vocal cords, which allows the compressed air to escape. The setting of the upper speech organs is dependent on that of the adjacent sounds. English [ʔ] may be used in the following cases:

(a) *Reinforcement of initial vowels.* – Accented words introduced by a vowel phoneme such as *always, every, iron* may be pronounced with an initial glottal stop (vocalic reinforcement): [ˈʔɔːlwɪz, ˈʔevrɪ, ˈʔaɪən], especially when additional emphasis is placed on the word.

(b) *Reinforcement of final voiceless stops.* – Some English speakers reinforce /p, t, tʃ, k/ in word-final position by a glottal closure, which will be perceived as a sudden interruption of the preceding sound. Words like *stop, that, watch, knock* may therefore be pronounced [stɒʔp, ðæʔt, wɒʔtʃ, nɒʔk]. This type of reinforcement is common when the following word begins with a consonant, cf. *stop crying, that girl, watch mother* and *knock-down*. A *replacement* of final /p, t, k/ by [ʔ] may even take place when a consonant follows. /t/ is much more frequently replaced than final /p, k/, especially before homorganic consonants (cf. *that table, not now*) but also before most other consonants (cf. *gatepost, nutmeg, not very*).

In Danish, glottal stops are frequently used to reinforce initial vowels in words such as *altid, ørken, Afrika*. A related phenomenon in Danish is the glottal sound called *stød*. The *stød* may occasionally be realised with glottal closure, for instance in exclamations (cf. *det fæ!* [feʔ]), but normally it is produced without any complete glottal closure. In contradistinction to the English glottal plosive, the Danish *stød* has a contrastive linguistic function, cf. the following Danish minimal pairs *mord-mor, ænder-ender, øget-øjet*, which all have *stød* in the first, but not in the second of the two words.

The glottal plosive is frequently used by native speakers of English and seems to be on the increase in educated speech. Although the glottal plosive is not a necessary feature of English, the Danish learner may use it in order to sound more authentically English, but should be careful not to transfer Danish *stød* patterns by using it with vowels and voiced consonants in such English words as *rob, hide, stage, beg*. Danes are particularly well advised to substitute the glottal plosive for word- or syllable-final /t/ before most consonants (cf. *get down, that chair, witness, football*). In this way they will not run the risk of replacing /t/ by /d/.

5.9. The distinction between voiced and voiceless fricatives

Above in § 5.3, English consonants were classified in two categories according to phonation: voiceless and voiced. The fricative phonemes belonging to the two classes are, respectively, /f, θ, s, ʃ, h/ and /v, ð, z, ʒ/. The voicing contrast does not apply to /h/, but the remaining fricatives can be grouped in four contrastive pairs: /f/ – /v/, /θ/ – /ð/, /s/ – /z/ and /ʃ/ – /ʒ/. As in the case of the stops (see above, § 5.6), voicelessness and voice are not the only properties by which the components of these pairs are distinguished. If again we whisper word pairs such as *fine-vine, thigh-thy, hiss-his*, and *ruche-rouge*, we can clearly hear the difference between the components of each pair. This suggests that voicing is just one among several factors that contribute to maintaining the distinction between /f, θ, s, ʃ/ and /v, ð, z, ʒ/. The following three phonetic properties enable us to distinguish between the two categories:

(1) *Force of articulation.* – /f, θ, s, ʃ/ are produced with greater force than /v, ð, z, ʒ/. The additional expenditure of energy shows itself in, among other things, greater duration, stronger airflow, more muscular tension and more noise.

(2) *Voicing.* – /f, θ, s, ʃ/ are always voiceless, but /v, ð, z, ʒ/ are often accompanied by voice. In medial position when occurring between voiced sounds, /v, ð, z, ʒ/ (in e.g. *evening, leather, buzzing, pleasure*) are fully voiced. In final position, for instance in *leave, breathe, expertise* and *prestige*, they are either weakly voiced with vocal-cord vibration only at the beginning or – and this is more frequent – completely voiceless. Initial /v, ð, z/ may be realised either with vocal-cord vibration towards the end of the sound or with full voice, cf. *very, than, zebra* (/ʒ/ does not occur initially in English).

(3) *Length of preceding sounds.* – When /f, θ, s, ʃ/ occur finally in the syllable, the length of a preceding vowel (or nasal or lateral) is considerably reduced. Accordingly, the vowels of *calf, sheath, dice, ruche* are relatively short, whereas in e.g. *carve, sheathe, dies, rouge* full vowel length is retained before final /v, ð, z, ʒ/. In medial position the length of vowels is also reduced; in, e.g., *rifle* and *racing* the vowels are somewhat shorter than in *rival* and *raising*.

Force of articulation always differentiates /f, θ, s, ʃ/ from /v, ð, z, ʒ/,[1] the relative contribution of the two remaining features as contrastive indicators being dependent on position in syllable and word according to the following pattern:

Initially in accented syllable. – In this position voicing (along with force of articulation) is the decisive factor:

| fan | thigh | seal | shy |
| van | thy | zeal | |

Medially, preceding unaccented syllable. – Voicing and length of preceding sounds in combination distinguish the two series in this position:

| rifle | Arthur | racer | pressure |
| rival | father | razor | pleasure |

Finally. – The decisive factor here is the reduction of the length of a preceding vowel (or nasal or lateral):

| life | wreath | ice | ruche |
| live (adj.) | wreathe | eyes | rouge |

5.10. The fricative phonemes

/f/

(1) *Articulation.* – This voiceless, labio-dental fricative is produced with an open glottis and a raised velum. The lower lip is raised and retracted, making

---

1. For this reason many phoneticians prefer the labels *fortis* (strong) and *lenis* (weak) about the two groups of consonants traditionally referred to as voiceless and voiced.

contact with the upper teeth so that the air escaping through the stricture causes friction.

(2) *Variation.* – There are no important allophonic variants of this phoneme.

(3) *Comparison with Danish.* – Whereas in Danish the articulation of [f] is sometimes rather lax, there is always firm contact at the place of articulation of the English equivalent, which is produced with vigorous retraction of the lower lip.

(4) *Spellings.* – /f/ is spelled with *f, ff* and *ph* as in *film*, *coffee*, and *photo*. In final and medial positions it may also be rendered by means of *gh* (*rough, laughing*).

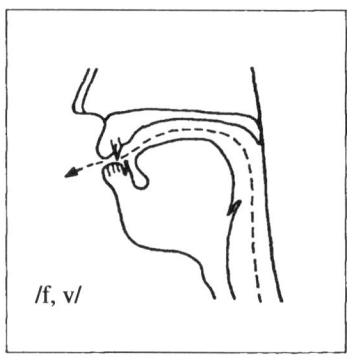

/v/

(1) *Articulation.* – /v/ is a voiced, labio-dental fricative. The setting of the organs of speech is identical with that of /f/ except that the vocal cords may vibrate.

(2) *Variation.* – Apart from devoiced [y] (cf. above, § 5.9) there are no important allophones of this phoneme.

(3) *Comparison with Danish.* – Having no contrast between [v] and [w], Danish has a [v] that is pronounced much less distinctly than the corresponding English fricative, i.e. without retraction of the lower lip and without friction. The Danish sound should therefore not be transferred to English. The Danish learner may acquire the English sound by retracting his lower lip, pushing it against the edge of his upper teeth and pressing the exhalation air through the firm stricture. Once he has learnt the correct sound, he will often have difficulty in using it in the appropriate places. In Danish, [v] is of rare occurrence in final and medial positions, written *v* in e.g. *skov, lov, over, hævne* being pronounced [u]; it is therefore important that the Danish learner takes care to pronounce English [v] correctly in these positions:

love	*over*
give	*devil*
move	*never*
sieve (/sɪv/)	*loving*
dove	*novel*

When he masters the sound in isolation and in individual words, he may go on by practising the pronunciation of such sequences as:

Every evening Vera would leave the naval base.
An inveterate vamp lived near the river.
Have the survivors saved the victuals?

(4) *Spellings.* – *v* is the regular orthographic rendering of /v/.

/θ/

(1) *Articulation.* – In the articulation of this voiceless, dental fricative the glottis is open and the velum raised. The tip of the tongue makes contact with the edge and back of the upper teeth, the surface of the tongue lying flat. Friction is produced as the air is pressed through the slit-like stricture. The lips are parted.

(2) *Variation.* – There are no important allophones af this phoneme.

(3) *Comparison with Danish.* – The consonantal system of Danish having no voiceless, dental fricative, Danes tend to replace /θ/ by the Danish consonant most closely related, /s/, in their pronunciation of such English words as *think, theory*. This constitutes a phonemic error, however, that may lead to misunderstanding. If, e.g., the replacement occurs in *think*, the word will be construed by speakers of English as *sink*. The Danish learner should therefore practise the pronunciation of word pairs containing the distinction between /θ/ and /s/:

thought	*sought*	*moth*	*moss*
thank	*sank*	*myth*	*miss*
thaw	*saw*	*truth*	*truce*
thin	*sin*	*mouth*	*mouse*
thunder	*sunder*	*tenth*	*tense*

Before *r* Danes are likely to substitute /t/ for /θ/. They should therefore distinguish carefully between /θ/ and /t/ in e.g. *through-true* and *thrill-trill*.

The learner may acquire the correct pronunciation of [θ] by putting out the tip of his tongue between his teeth, the air escaping between the tip of the tongue and the upper teeth. When he has acquired such an interdental [θ], he may retract the tip of his tongue a little. Even after mastering the sound in isolation, he will probably still have difficulty in pronouncing it in combination with voiced and voiceless *s*-sounds:

/θ/ + /s/	/θ/ + /z/	/s/ + /θ/	/z/ + /θ/
moths	*both zebras*	*this theatre*	*his thigh*
births	*the south zone*	*Nick's theory*	*those thistles*
months	*the fifth Zulu*	*nice things*	*he's threatening*

Longer sequences may be used for practising the pronunciation of /θ/:

Both theories of thermodynamics are worthless.
The wound in Ruth's throat was throbbing with pain.
The third thief was no athlete.
The moon's path round the earth

(4) *Spellings.* – /θ/ is always spelled with *th*.

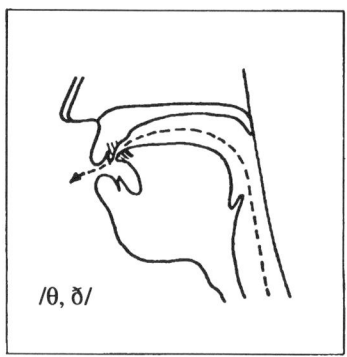

/ð/

(1) *Articulation.* – /ð/ is a voiced, dental fricative. The setting of the organs of speech is identical with that of /θ/ except that the vocal cords may vibrate.

(2) *Variation.* – Apart from devoiced [ð̥] (cf. above, § 5.9) there are no important allophonic variants of /ð/.

(3) *Comparison with Danish.* – Danish words such as *bide, bad* exhibit a voiced fricative which is related to English [ð] and is transcribed in phonetic script by means of the same symbol. In the articulation of Danish [ð] there is a lax stricture between the blade/front of the tongue and the alveolar ridge. The tongue-tip, which is raised in the production of English [ð], remains lowered. Since English and Danish [ð] diverge with regard to both the active and passive articulators and to the degree of firmness of articulation, it is evident that the Danish sound is too different from its English counterpart to allow it to be transferred to English.

The best way for the learner to acquire the correct pronunciation of /ð/ would be to put his tongue between his teeth, exhaling air and adding voice at the same time. When he has learnt to pronounce a strongly articulated, interdental [ð], he may gradually retract the tip of the tongue a little. Even after mastering the sound in isolation, he will frequently have additional difficulties in pronouncing it in connection with voiced and voiceless *s*-sounds:

/ð/ + /z/	/ð/ + /s/	/z/ + /ð/	/s/ + /ð/
paths	*soothe Simon*	*please them*	*miss those*
mouths	*smoothe silk*	*graze there*	*nice there*
loathes	*withstand*	*needs them*	*eats that*

Longer sequences may be used for practising the pronunciation of [ð]:

Their mother and father gathered the clothes together.
They breathed the soothing air during the smooth crossing.
My brother loathes this weather.

(4) *Spellings.* – /ð/ is always spelled with *th*.

/s/

(1) *Articulation.* – This voiceless, alveolar fricative is produced with an open glottis and a raised velum. The tip and blade of the tongue make contact with the alveolar ridge, the side rims of the tongue being raised so that there is a narrow groove in the centre of the tongue. The air escaping along this groove-shaped stricture and hitting the teeth, causes strong and hissing friction. The lips are parted.

(2) *Variation.* – There are no important allophones of /s/.

(3) *Comparison with Danish.* – Danish [s] may be transferred to English.

(4) *Spellings.* – /s/ is spelled with *s*, *ss* as in *say*, *lesson* and with *c* when this letter is followed by the written vowels *e*, *i*, *y* as in *face*, *cider*, *cyst*. In *island*, *isle*, and *viscount* there is no [s].

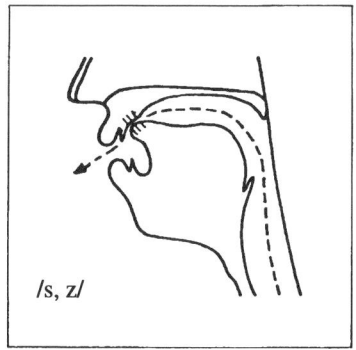

/z/

(1) *Articulation.* – /z/ is a voiced, alveolar fricative. The setting of the speech organs is identical with that of /s/ except that the vocal cords may vibrate.

(2) *Variation.* – The only important allophone is devoiced [z̥] (cf. above, § 5.9).

(3) *Comparison with Danish.* – Danish having no voiced, alveolar fricative, Danes tend to replace [z] by [s] in their pronunciation of words such as *zoo* and *zebra*. This is a phonemic error, however, that may lead to misunderstanding. If for instance the replacement occurs in the word *zeal*, it will be construed by speakers of English as *seal*. The Danish learner must therefore train himself in identifying mini-

mal pairs such as those listed below and in reproducing them by voicing [z] distinctly in initial and medial positions, by reducing the length of sounds preceding [s] medially and especially finally, and by articulating [s] with more force than [z] in all positions:

/z/	/s/	/z/	/s/	/z/	/s/
zip	*sip*	*causes*	*courses*	*eyes*	*ice*
zone	*sown*	*losing*	*loosing*	*dies*	*dice*
zinc	*sink*	*razor*	*racer*	*pens*	*pence*

Should the Danish learner have difficulty in acquiring English [z] and in distinguishing between this sound and [s], he is well advised to take as his starting point the only voicing contrast familiar to him from his own language, viz. [f] - [v]. By saying [fvfvfvfv...] without altering the setting of his upper speech organs, he will improve his skill in adding and removing voice, a skill that he may transfer to the *s*-sounds by saying [szszszsz...] with the upper speech organs set in the same position. He may also practise the pronunciation of [z] by singing the sound. Once he has learnt [z], the Danish learner is likely to exaggerate his use of voice, making the sound too buzzing. Pedagogically misguided efforts may lead students to overdo the degree of voicing in final position, where it sounds particularly un-English.

The following long sequences may be used for practising the pronunciation of [z]:

> *Dozens of grazing zebras*
> *The zealous boys poisoned the prisoners.*
> *He was gazing at the weasels behind the bars.*
> *A vase with a dismal design of flowers*
> *A pleasant seaside resort with roses*

(4) *Spellings.* – /z/ is regularly spelled with *s*, *z* and *zz* as in *busy*, *zone* and *dizzy*.

/ʃ/

(1) *Articulation.* – In the articulation of this voiceless, palato-alveolar fricative the glottis is open and the velum raised. The tip, blade and front of the tongue make contact with the alveolar ridge and front part of the hard palate, the side rims of the tongue being raised so that there is a groove in the centre of the tongue. The air escaping through this groove-shaped stricture causes strong and sizzling friction. It should be noted that the friction occurs over a more extensive area of articulation than in the case of [s] and that the articulation of [ʃ] is laxer than that of [s]. The lips are rounded.

(2) *Variation.* – There are no important allophones of this phoneme.

(3) *Comparison with Danish.* – Danish /ʃ/ in, e.g., *sjakre*, *sjofel*, *sjusk* is normally realised as a single sound, [ʃ], but some speakers of standard Danish use the cluster [sj] instead. Danish thus has free variation between [ʃ] and [sj]. This is not paral-

lelled in English, where [ʃ] is the only possibility in words like *shade* and *shallow* with the initial phoneme /ʃ/ (spelled *sh*). Conversely, [ʃ] does not occur in *suit*, *suicide* which may be pronounced either with the initial sequence /sj/ or with /s/. Because of the free variation in Danish between [ʃ] and [sj] and the difficulty that a strict distinction between the two may present to Danes, the Danish learner is well advised to avoid the English cluster /sj/ altogether in words like *suicide*, *sue*, *superb*, seeing that the majority of speakers of standard English use initial /s/ in such cases. In e.g. *assume* and *consume* /sj/ is preferred by most standard speakers, but since /s/ is by no means stigmatized even in such cases, it is better for the Danish learner to stick to /s/ rather than produce an un-English realisation of /sj/ or make a direct phonemic error.

The correct pronunciation of English [ʃ], which is not identical with the Danish sound, may be acquired in the following manner: The lips should be rounded and pushed forward, the tongue being lax. The exhalation of air through the stricture will produce strong and sizzling friction that has a deeper quality than in the case of [s]. Once the sound is mastered in isolation and in individual words, the learner may go on by practising examples such as:

> *The Russian ships could be seen fishing off the French seashore.*
> *That marshal is surely ambitious and ferocious.*
> *A posh Welshman with moustache and galoshes*

(4) *Spellings.* – /ʃ/ is regularly spelled with *sh*. In two extraordinary cases, *sure* and *sugar*, /ʃ/ is rendered orthographically by *s*.

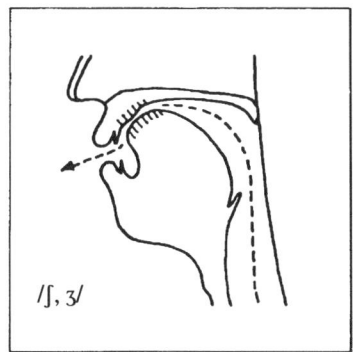

/ʒ/

(1) *Articulation.* – /ʒ/ is a voiced, palato-alveolar fricative. The setting of the speech organs is identical with that of /ʃ/ except that the vocal cords may vibrate.

(2) *Variation.* – The only important allophone is devoiced [ʒ̊] (cf. above, § 5.9).

(3) *Comparison with Danish.* – In the consonantal system of Danish there is no voiced, palato-alveolar fricative. It is therefore difficult for Danes to perceive and

render this consonant, the usual Danish replacement for /ʒ/ being /ʃ/, cf. the erroneous pronunciation of e.g. *pleasure*: ['pleʃə].

The correct pronunciation of /ʒ/ may be achieved by voicing [ʃ]. If this creates any problems, the Danish learner may take the well-known voicing contrast between [f] and [v] as his point of departure and practise the pronunciation of [ʃʒʃʒʃʒ...], the upper speech organs being set in the same position. The learner may also profitably sing [ʒ]. Once he has learnt [ʒ], he should take care not to overdo voicing in final position. Even if the difference between [ʒ] and [ʃ] rarely has a contrastive function, it is important to be able to distinguish the two phonemes and distribute them correctly in words such as:

/ʃ/	/ʒ/	/ʃ/	/ʒ/
fission	vision	ruche	rouge
pressure	pleasure	moustache	camouflage
nation	evasion	leash	prestige

Longer sequences may be used for practising the pronunciation of [ʒ]:

Their decision to use balloon barrage
He had a vision of a treasure in his garage.
I have no illusions about any invasion of Bruges.
On rare occasions Carol took pleasure in her beige dress.

(4) *Spellings*. – In medial position /ʒ/ is spelled with, *si, zi, s(u), z(u)* as in *invasion, glazier, closure, seizure* and in final position with *ge* as in *prestige*.

/h/

(1) *Articulation*. – This voiceless, glottal fricative is produced with a raised velum. The glottis is open, and there is free passage of air through the oral cavity and between the lips. A strong airflow is expelled through the open speech channel, producing friction in the upper cavities and also frequently in the open glottis. The lips and tongue are shaped in readiness for the following vowel.

(2) *Variation*. – /h/ is realised as a voiceless fricative anticipating a following vowel. Consequently there are as many allophones af /h/ as there are vowels in English, cf. the three different [h]-sounds in *heat, heart, hoot*.

(3) *Comparison with Danish*. – [h] is pronounced and distributed in English in the same way as it is in Danish. Only the cluster /hj/ in e.g. *huge* (/hju:dʒ/), being unfamiliar to most Danes, will present any difficulty to the Danish learner.

(4) *Spellings*. – /h/ is regularly spelled with *h* and occasionally with *wh* as in *horse, who*. In *hour, honour, vehicle*, etc. there is no [h].

5.11. The nasals

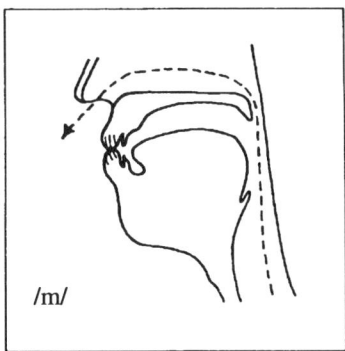

/m/

(1) *Articulation.* – In the pronunciation of this bilabial nasal the lower lip is raised, forming a closure with the upper lip. The vocal cords vibrate, and the velum is lowered, enabling the airflow to pass through the nose continuously.

(2) *Variation.* – [m] is shortened by a following voiceless consonant as in *dump*. Otherwise there are no important allophones of /m/.

(3) *Comparison with Danish.* – Initially and medially there is no difference between English and Danish in the way [m] is pronounced. Consequently, there are no problems in learning the English sound. In final position the pronunciation of [m] is short in Danish but relatively long in English, compare Danish *kom, dum* with English *come, dumb*. Accordingly, Danish [m] should not be transferred to English in final position without being lengthened.

(4) *Spellings.* – /m/ is regularly spelled with *m* and frequently with *mm* as in *measles* and *hammer*.

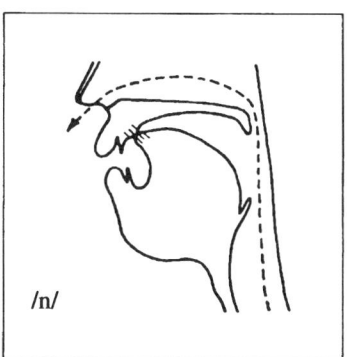

/n/

(1) *Articulation.* – In the articulation of this alveolar nasal the tip of the tongue is raised, forming a closure with the alveolar ridge. The lips are parted, the vocal cords vibrate and the velum is lowered, enabling the airflow to pass through the nose continuously.

(2) *Variation.* – [n] is shortened by a following voiceless consonant as in *sent* or *since* (in contrast with *send* or *sin, sins*). Before a dental sound, as in *tenth*, the articulation is dental rather than alveolar.

(3) *Comparison with Danish.* – Initially and medially Danish [n] may be transferred to English without any alteration. In final position, however, it is shorter than English [n], compare Danish *tin* with English *tin*. Lengthening is therefore required in this position.

(4) *Spellings.* – /n/ is regularly spelled with *n* and frequently with *nn* as in *nasal* and *sinner*. In e.g. *damn* and *hymn* there is no [n].

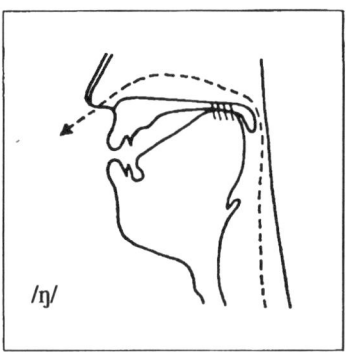

/ŋ/

(1) *Articulation.* – In the articulation of this velar nasal the back of the tongue is raised, forming a closure with the velum. The lips are parted, the vocal cords vibrate, and the velum is lowered enabling the airflow to pass through the nose continuously.

(2) *Variation.* – The precise place of articulation depends on the quality of adjacent vowels: there is palatal closure after front vowels (*ring*) and velar closure after central and back vowels (*young, throng*). Auditorily there is barely any difference between these allophones. [ŋ] is shortened by a following voiceless consonant as in *sink* (in contrast with *sing*).

(3) *Comparison with Danish.* – Medial Danish [ŋ] may be directly transferred to English. In final position, however, Danish [ŋ] is shorter than its English counterpart, compare Danish *lang* with English *lung*. Lengthening is therefore required in final position.

(4) *Spellings.* – /ŋ/ is regularly spelled with *ng* and with *n* followed by a letter representing a velar stop, cf. *wrong, finger, link, anchor, uncle*.

5.12. The liquids

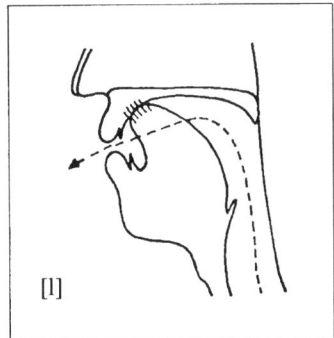
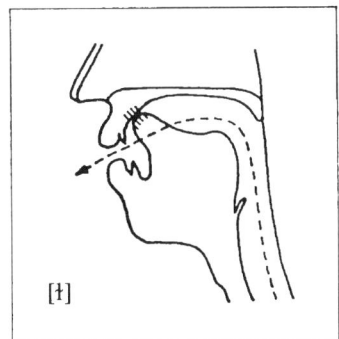

/l/

(1) *Articulation.* – In the articulation of this lateral liquid the velum is raised and the vocal cords vibrate. The tip of the tongue is raised, making contact with the alveolar ridge. The exhalation air, which can escape along one or both sides of the tongue, passes through the mouth continuously. The lips are parted.

(2) *Variation.* – The two most important allophonic variants of this phoneme are clear [l] and dark [ɫ]. The difference between the two allophones depends on how the tongue is shaped behind the place of articulation. For clear [l], the front of the tongue is raised a little in the direction of the hard palate; for dark [ɫ], the back of the tongue is raised in the direction of the soft palate, the tongue position resembling that of the vowel [ʊ]. It should be noted that the two allophones share the same chief place of articulation (alveolar ridge). In auditory terms, [ɫ] diverges from [l] in having a darker and deeper (more velarised) resonance. The two allophones are distributed according to the following rule:

/l/ → [l] before vowels and /j/, e.g. *love, stallion* (['stæljən]).
/l/ → [ɫ] before consonants (minus /j/), finally and when syllabic, e.g. *bulk, hill, battle* (['bætɫ]).

A word like *lull* ([lʌɫ]) shows how [l] typically occurs initially and [ɫ] in final position.

A third important allophone is devoiced [l̥] which occurs after /p/ and /k/ in accented syllables, e.g. in *play* and *clue*.

Before a dental sound, as in *health*, the articulation is dental rather than alveolar.

(3) *Comparison with Danish.* – The Danish consonant [l] is auditorily almost identical with English clear [l] and may consequently be transferred to English in words such as *light, million*, etc. But Danes also substitute their [l] for dark [ɫ] in words like

call, milk, cattle, and their English interlocutors will find this pronunciation un-English or at least non-standard. In order to acquire the correct pronunciation of [ɫ] the learner should take clear [l] as his starting point and at the same time raise the back of his tongue in the direction of the soft palate. A strategy for learning this additional articulation would be to pronounce [l] and [u:] simultaneously. The following long sequences may be used for practising the pronunciation of [ɫ]:

> *Bill sold his old poodle.*
> *The bottle is full of scalding milk.*
> *Saul was partial to tall, pale girls.*

Once the learner has acquired the pronunciation of both [l] and [ɫ], he may practise the correct distribution of the two allophones, using sentences that contain both [l] and [ɫ]:

> *Little Laura blushed and then turned pale.*
> *It is illegal to peddle in this village.*

In final position the realisation of /l/ is not only dark but also long (cf. our discussion of final nasals above in § 5.11). The lateral is considerably longer in, e.g., English *well* than in Danish *vel*. Accordingly Danish [l] should not be transferred in this position, neither in relation to quality nor to quantity. [ɫ] is shortened by a following voiceless consonant as in *help* (in contrast with *hell*).

(4) Spellings. – /l/ is regularly spelled with *l* and *ll* as in *laugh* and *bell*. In *talk, walk, half, calf, calm, could, should*, etc. there is no [l].

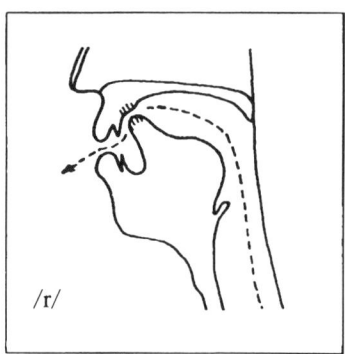

/r/

(1) *Articulation.* – This non-lateral liquid is produced with a raised velum and vibrating vocal cords. The tip of the tongue is raised, being very near to but not touching the back of the alveolar ridge. The exhalation air escapes freely through the mouth. Behind the place of articulation there is a hollow in the surface of the tongue. The lips are rounded.

(2) *Variation.* – When following /p, t, k/ in accented syllables, /r/ is devoiced ([r̥]), and friction arises, cf. e.g. *pray, tray, cray-fish.* In highly stylized speech (in the declamation of poetry, etc.) /r/ is realised as a lingual trill. This is a free variant that is produced by letting the tip vibrate against the alveolar ridge in a strong airflow.

At this point we should introduce the phenomenon known as *linking r.* When a word ending in a written *r* or *re* is immediately followed by a grammatically closely related word beginning with a vowel, most English speakers will insert an *r*-sound. Cases in point are when the word *far*, which is pronounced [fɑː] in isolation, is followed by *off* (/ˈfɑːr ˈɒf/) and when the words *four* and *father*, which have no *r*-sounds when said in isolation, are joined together with, respectively, *eggs*, and *in-law* to form the combinations /ˈfɔːr ˈegz/ and /ˈfɑːðər ɪn lɔː/.

(3) *Comparison with Danish.* – Danish words like *råbe* and *reb* have a uvular *r*, which has a degree of auditory relationship with the tongue-tip *r* of English. This fricative sound, which is denoted with [ʁ], is produced by means of a stricture comprising the back and root of the tongue on the one hand and the uvula and pharyngeal wall on the other. Obviously, the Danish sound cannot be transferred to English seeing that it diverges from the English sound with regard to both place and manner of articulation. The substitution of uvular [ʁ] for [r] sounds very un-English and will immediately give the speaker away as a foreigner.

If a Danish learner finds it difficult to abandon [ʁ] he will be pedagogically well advised to regard English [r] as a completely new and unfamiliar kind of sound instead of looking at it as a type of *r* that is related to the Danish sound. If the learner masters the pronunciation of [w] (see below, § 5.13), he may take this sound as his starting point, and subsequently raise the tip of his tongue in the direction of the alveolar ridge. A word like *red* may first be rendered as [wed] and then changed to [red] by raising the tongue-tip. Another approach would be to raise the tip of the tongue to the alveolar ridge, lower the tip a little, and then articulate the vowel [ɜː] as in *err.* Once the learner masters such a modified [ɜː], he may use it initially in words like *right* and *wrong.*

The following long sequences may be used for practising the pronunciation of [r]:

> *Robert promised to try a dry martini.*
> *A very rare red rose*
> *An arrogant rogue arrived last Friday.*
> *Ralph was run over by a road-roller.*
> *The Romans were forced to retreat but threatened revenge.*

(4) *Spellings.* – /r/ is regularly spelled with *r* and *rr* as in *realm* and *carry.*

5.13. The semi-vowels

/w/

(1) *Articulation.* – This labial-velar semi-vowel is produced with a raised velum and vibrating vocal cords. The lips are pushed forward and closely rounded, the back of

the tongue being raised in the direction of the velum approximately as in [ʊ]. It should be noted that there are two strictures of equal rank in the speech channel – between the upper and the lower lips and between the back of the tongue and the velum – and it is this double articulation that is denoted by the term labial-velar.

(2) *Variation.* – When following /k/ and /t/ in accented syllables, /w/ is devoiced ([w̥]) and labial friction arises, cf. e.g. *queen* and *twin*.

(3) *Comparison with Danish.* – The consonantal system of Danish has no labial-velar semi-vowel, Danes replacing /w/ by the phonetically closely related Danish consonant /v/ in words like *work* and *wing*. This is a phonemic error, however, which may lead to misunderstanding. If the substitution takes place in e.g. *wail*, the word will be construed in English as *veil*. It is consequently important for the learner to train himself in perceiving and rendering the distinction between /w/ and /v/ in word pairs such as:

while	*vile*	*wheel*	*veal*
worse	*verse*	*whack*	*vac*
wine	*vine*	*wane*	*vain*
west	*vest*	*wary*	*vary*

The correct pronunciation of [w] may be acquired by first replacing it by [u:] and then reducing the vowel. The learner should start out by rendering *whim* and *wag* as [u:ɪm] and [u:æg] and subsequently shorten them to [wɪm] and [wæg]. Once he masters the sound in isolation and in individual words, he may practise the pronunciation of longer sequences such as:

Williams was walking warily.
The waves washed the cliffs away.
We wearied Walter with requests.
A warm welcome awaited us.
My squaw is waiting in the wigwam.

When he has acquired [w], he may practise the alternation between [w] and [v] in sentences such as:

Vera knew the queen's nephew very well.
Will he behave well during the voyage?
Have we invited the veterans from Worcester?

(4) *Spellings.* – /w/ is regularly spelled with *w* as in *well* and with *wh*, *(q)u* as in *whisky*, *quest*. In *wrap*, *wrestle*, *wrong* and *who*, *whole*, *two*, *answer*, etc. there is no [w].

/j/

(1) *Articulation.* – In the pronunciation of this palatal semi-vowel the velum is raised and the vocal cords vibrate. The lips are parted, the front of the tongue being raised towards the hard palate approximately as in [ɪ].

(2) *Variation.* – When following /p, t, k, h/ in accented syllables, /j/ is devoiced ([j̊]) and palatal friction arises, cf. e.g. *pewter, tunic, curious, human.*

(3) *Comparison with Danish.* – There is no difference between the English and Danish pronunciation of [j]. Consequently the sound presents no problems to the Danish learner.

(4) *Spellings.* – /j/ is regularly spelled with *y* and frequently with *i* as in *yacht* (/jɒt/) and *million* (/'mɪljən/).

(5) *Note.* – After the consonants /θ, s, z, l/ there is vacillation between /juː/ and /uː/. Words like *enthusiasm, super, presume, lunacy* may be pronounced with either (/ɪn'θ(j)uːzɪæzm, 's(j)uːpə, prɪ'z(j)uːm, 'l(j)uːnəsɪ/). In other cases /j/ is retained, including after /n, d, t/, as in *new* (/njuː/), *due* (/djuː/), *tune* (/tjuːn/).

6. THE ENGLISH VOWELS

6.1. Description of the vowels

Above, it was mentioned that in the articulation of vowels there is approximation between two organs in the speech tract, but that the active articulator does not touch the passive articulator along the centre line of the mouth (cf. § 1.2 and § 5.1). Unlike consonants, vowels thus exhibit no well-defined area of contact that we may use as a convenient starting point for our articulatory description, vowels being consequently more difficult to describe than consonants. Whereas, e.g., the consonant [f] may be immediately described on the basis of its labio-dental area of contact, which may be felt as well as observed, it is much more difficult to describe in articulatory terms how, e.g., the vowel [ɔ:] (as in English *ball*) is pronounced. It is due to such difficulties that the vowels of a foreign language – to a much higher degree than its consonants – must be acquired through *imitation*, a point of 'diminishing returns' being reached much more rapidly in the articulatory description of vowels than in that of consonants.

Different vowel qualities may be produced by modifying the shape of the speech tract, and since such modifications are mainly achieved by movement of the tongue, the description of vowel sounds must account for the position of the tongue. In the first place it must be noted what part of the surface of the tongue is raised towards the roof of the mouth. Taking *place of articulation* as our point of departure, we may distinguish between front, central and back vowels as exemplified by /i:/, /ɜ:/ and /ɔ:/, cf. English *bead*, *bird*, and *board*. Secondly, we must determine the degree to which the tongue is raised, and we operate with four *tongue heights*: close, half-close, half-open and open, cf. /u:/, /ʊ/, /ɔ:/ and /ɑ:/ in English *food*, *hood*, *board* and *hard*.

The following two profiles show the approximate tongue positions characteristic of the vowels in the Danish words *mile, mele, mæle, male* and *mule, mole, måle, Maren*:

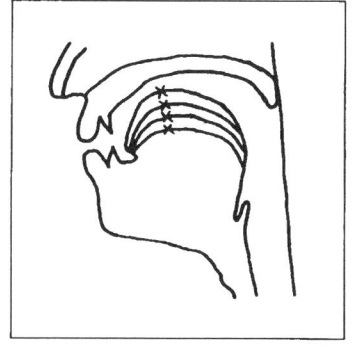 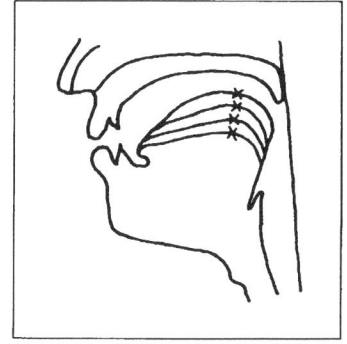

Front vowels (Danish) Back vowels (Danish)
[i:]   [u:]
[e:]   [o:]
[ɛ:]   [ɔ:]
[a:]   [ɑ:]

In addition to tongue position it is relevant also to describe the lip position: when the lips are rounded (and therefore protruded), both the size of the oral aperture and the length of the speech channel are modified so as to influence the quality of vowels decisively. A distinction is made between rounded and unrounded vowels, cf. e.g. /y:/ and /i:/ in Danish *kyle* and *kile*.

By operating with three places of articulation, four tongue heights and two lip positions, we are able to distinguish 24 vowel sounds, which will be enough to provide a rough description of the vowels of a given language. As in the case of the consonants, we may summarize our phonetic descriptions of vowels, characterizing for example Danish /i/ as an unrounded, close front vowel and Danish /o/ as a rounded, half-close back vowel.

Finally, the importance of distinguishing between *long* and *short* vowels (cf. /i:/ and /i/ in Danish *hvile* og *ville*) and between *monophthongs* and *diphthongs* should be stressed. A diphthong combines two vowel elements in one syllable, cf. /ai/ in Danish *rejse*.

However, the method just discussed with its mere 24 vowel sounds is inadequate when finer and more accurate descriptions are needed. In such circumstances vowels can be described through comparison with a set of *cardinal vowels*, a system devised by the English phonetician Daniel Jones. Being arbitrarily selected vowel sounds, these cardinal vowels do not belong to any language in particular and serve only as a frame of reference for specific vowel descriptions. Jones established his set of cardinal vowels by means of the following procedure: for the pronunciation of [i] he raised the front of his tongue as close as possible to the hard palate without any friction occurring; then, for the cardinal vowel [ɑ], he lowered and retracted his tongue as much as possible without pharyngeal friction being produced. Lowering the front of the tongue from the position of [i], he pronounced the three vowels [e], [ɛ] and [a] in such a way that auditorily they gave the impression of having equi-distant tongue heights. Similarly, he raised the back of his tongue from [ɑ], producing the three cardinal vowels [ɔ], [o] and [u], which also seemed to be auditorily equi-distant. Thus only two of the eight cardinal vowels have a physiological basis, while the remaining six were established by means of auditory judgments. However, X-ray photographs have confirmed the spatial relationships of the six vowels. Jones's original recording of the cardinal vowels provides us with a yardstick that may be applied to any type of vowel description.

To give a visual representation of the relationship of a given vowel to the cardinal vowels, we may plot the vowel in a highly conventionalized diagram which is based on the cardinal vowel tongue positions with front vowels to the left, back vowels to the right, close vowels at the top and open ones at the bottom. Any existent or conceivable vowel may be plotted on this chart. By way of illustration, the position of the English vowel [ɪ] is indicated in the cardinal vowel diagram:

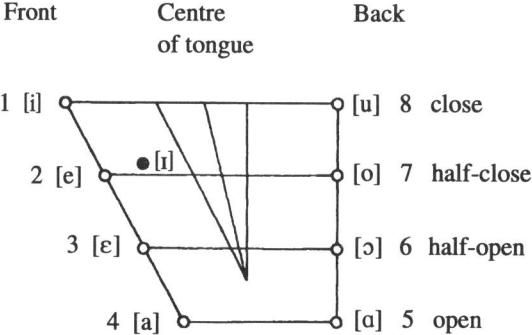

It should be noted that this system is only two-dimensional, lip rounding being not indicated. Cardinal vowels nos. 1-5 are unrounded, the rest being rounded. This method of presentation is motivated by the fact that most languages have unrounded front vowels and rounded back (other than fully open) vowels.

6.2. The inventory of vowel phonemes

As in the case of the consonants, the inventory of vowel phonemes can be established by means of positing series of words which are minimally different. As mentioned above in § 5.1, the vowels are central units, and we must therefore identify the number of contrastive units occurring in the central position of the syllable. A single list of words such as *lead, lid, lead* (metal), *lad, Lud, lard, lord, looed, laid, lied, Lloyd, load, loud, leered, laird* and *lured* supplies us with a stock of no fewer than 16 commutable, syllable-central units: /iː, ɪ, e, æ, ʌ, ɑː, ɔː, uː, eɪ, aɪ, ɔɪ, əʊ, aʊ, ɪə, eə, ʊə/. A second series of words that are minimally different, *hod, hood, heard, heed, hid, head, had, hard, hoard, hide*, adds another three vowels to our provisional inventory: /ɒ, ʊ, ɜː/. By inserting different speech sounds in different phonetic sequences, we have been able to show that there are 19 vowel phonemes in *accented* position. By investigating also vowel sounds in *unaccented* syllables, we may add yet another vowel phoneme to our stock of units, /ə/, cf. minimal pairs like *rudder* (/ˈrʌdə/) ≠ *ruddy* (/ˈrʌdɪ/) and *armour* (/ˈɑːmə/) ≠ *army* (/ˈɑːmɪ/). We thus arrive at a total of 20 which constitute the final inventory of vowel phonemes. Below, a list of these contrastive, syllable-central units is given:

/iː/	/liːd/	lead	/ɜː/	/hɜːd/	heard
/ɪ/	/lɪd/	lid	/ʌ/	/lʌd/	Lud
/e/	/led/	lead	/eɪ/	/leɪd/	laid
/æ/	/læd/	lad	/aɪ/	/laɪd/	lied
/ɑː/	/lɑːd/	lard	/ɔɪ/	/lɔɪd/	Lloyd
/ɒ/	/hɒd/	hod	/əʊ/	/ləʊd/	load
/ɔː/	/lɔːd/	lord	/aʊ/	/laʊd/	loud
/ʊ/	/hʊd/	hood	/ɪə/	/lɪəd/	leered
/uː/	/luːd/	looed	/eə/	/leəd/	laird
/ə/	/ˈrʌdə/	rudder	/ʊə/	/lʊəd/	lured

6.3. The system of vowels

Having established the English vowel inventory, our next step is a *classification* of the units represented and an investigation of their *systemic* interrelations. We shall therefore describe the phonetic features that are especially important and which keep the vowels distinct.

In accordance with their *stability of articulation* the English vowels may be assigned to two general categories: *monophthongs* and *diphthongs*. In the articulation of diphthongs like /aɪ/ and /aʊ/ in *find* and *found*, there is a distinct glide from one vowel position to another. Monophthongs such as /e/ and /ɜ:/ in *head* and *heard* are relatively stable, being produced without such a glide from one vowel position to another.

As far as *place of articulation* is concerned, both monophthongs and diphthongs can be divided into three subgroups. Monophthongs thus fall into *front vowels* (/i:, ɪ, e, æ/), *central vowels* (/ɜ:, ə, ʌ/) and *back vowels* (/u:, ʊ, ɔ:, ɒ, ɑ:/). As regards diphthongs, they are most conveniently classified in accordance with their second elements. We may consequently distinguish between diphthongs whose second elements are, respectively, half-close front vowels, half-close back vowels and central vowels, and which may therefore be described as *front-closing, back-closing* and *centring* diphthongs. In the articulation of the front-closing diphthongs (/eɪ, aɪ, ɔɪ/) there is a glide towards /ɪ/, in that of the back-closing ones (/əʊ, aʊ/) a glide towards /ʊ/, and finally, in the pronunciation of the centring diphthongs (/ɪə, eə, ʊə/), there is a glide moving towards /ə/, i.e. towards a central vowel position:

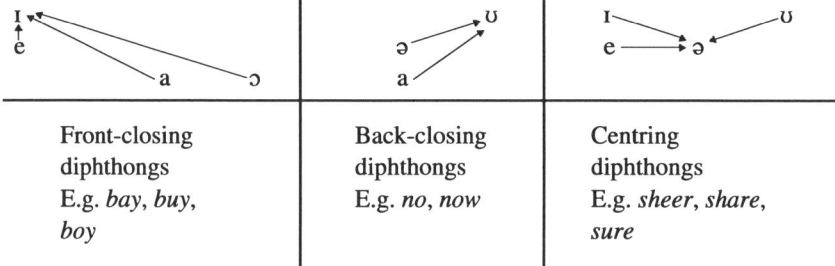

| Front-closing diphthongs E.g. *bay, buy, boy* | Back-closing diphthongs E.g. *no, now* | Centring diphthongs E.g. *sheer, share, sure* |

Monophthongs (and the component parts of diphthongs) may also be classified according to their *degree of raising* (tongue height) as *close* (/i:, u:/), *half close* (/ɪ, ʊ/), *half open* (/e, ɜ:, ə, ɔ:/) and *open* (/æ, ʌ, ɑ:, ɒ/) vowel sounds. The classifications of the English monophthongs so far may be summarized by means of the following diagram:

Tongue height	Place of articulation		
	Front	Central	Back
Close	i:		u:
Half-close	ɪ		ʊ
Half-open	e	ɜ:, ə	ɔ:
Open	æ	ʌ	ɑ:, ɒ

However, this table does not distinguish /ɜ:/ from /ə/ (both half-open central vowels) nor /ɑ:/ from /ɒ/ (both open back vowels), so we need an additional distinction. Both /ɜ:/ and /ɑ:/ differ in relative length from their counterparts with the same place of articulation and degree of raising, and we may therefore make a classification according to *vowel length* (or *quantity*). Our category of *long* vowels thus embraces the monophthongs /i:, ɑ:, ɔ:, u:, ɜ:/ along with all the diphthongs, our category of *short* vowels comprising the monophthongs /ɪ, e, æ, ʌ, ɒ, ʊ, ə/.

Using the three criteria of classification discussed above, we may now tabulate the English monophthongs in the following manner:

	Short			Long		
	Front	Central	Back	Front	Central	Back
Close				i:		u:
Half-close	ɪ		ʊ			
Half-open	e	ə			ɜ:	ɔ:
Open	æ	ʌ	ɒ			ɑ:

In this system each vowel is delimited from the rest by means of a three-dimensional phonetic classification. According to this classification, /ɑ:/ may for instance be described as a long, open back vowel, /ə/ as a short, half-open central vowel, /i:/ as a long, close front vowel, etc. The fact that both place of articulation, tongue height and quantity are significant phonetic features in English, can be demonstrated by means of pairs such as /hæt/ (*hat*) – /hʌt/ (*hut*) which differ merely in terms of place of articulation, /bet/ (*bet*) – /bæt/ (*bat*) which differ only in degree of tongue height, and /ˈfɔ:wɜ:d/ (*foreword*) – /ˈfɔ:wəd/ (*forward*) where vowel length (quantity) is the primary differentiating factor.

In § 6.1 above, we emphasized the importance of *rounding* for the phonetic quality of vowels, and this holds true also of English. However, it should be noted that despite the bearing rounding has on vowel quality, no English vowel is distinguished solely by means of rounding (unlike what is the case in Danish, cf. *kile* ≠ *kyle*). The components of the pairs /i:/ ≠ /u:/, /ɪ/ ≠ /ʊ/ and /ɜ:/ ≠ /ɔ:/ differ not only in lip rounding but also in their place of articulation while /ɑ:/ ≠ /ɒ/ are also differentiated in terms of quantity.

Let us finally summarize our classification of the English vowels according to distinctive phonetic features by means of the following diagram depicting the entire vowel system:

Long monophthongs		Short monophthongs		Diphthongs
i:	u:	ɪ	ʊ	ɪ ʊ
ɜ:	ɔ:	e ə		e — ə
	ɑ:	æ ʌ	ɒ	a ɔ

It might be added that short accented monophthongs only appear in closed syllables, i.e. when followed by consonants, as in /pɪt, pet, pæt, pʌt, pɒt, pʊt/ (*pit, pet, pat, putt, pot, put*). Conversely, long monophthongs and diphthongs occur in both (accented) open and closed syllables, cf. such examples as /hiː, haɪ/ (*he, high*) and /hiːd, haɪd/ (*heed, hide*).

6.4. Comparison with Danish

Having established the vowel phonemes of English and described their systemic interrelations, we shall now make a comparison between English and Danish in order to uncover the differences between the vowels of the two languages and to identify the difficulties of pronunciation that the Danish learner will come across.

There are 13 short monophthongs and 12 long monophthongs in Standard Danish. The short monophthongs are /i, e, ɛ, y, ø, œ, a, ɑ, ɒ, ɔ, o, u, ə/ as exemplified by the following series of words: *mit, midt, mæt, nyt, mødt, søn, mat, rat, vor, godt, kul, mut,* and *galde* (/ˈgalə/). The long monophthongs /iː, eː, ɛː, yː, øː, œː, aː, ɑː, ɒː, ɔː, oː, uː/ are qualitatively closely related to the short ones and are consequently denoted by the same symbols ([o] and [ɔ], however, being somewhat more open than [oː] and [ɔː]). As instances of this group of vowels we may cite the words *mile, mele, mæle, syle, søle, høne, male, Maren, morgen, måle, mole,* and *mule*. The Danish diphthongs /ai, ɔi; au, œu; iɒ, ɛɒ, uɒ/ (as attested in *sejle, søjle; savle, høvle; kirke, lærke* and *purke*) are, respectively, front-closing, back-closing and back-opening.

The Danish and English *monophthongs* may be compared by means of the two diagrams given below:

	English			Danish		
	Front	Central	Back	Front	Central	Back
Close	iː		uː	i, iː y, yː		u, uː
Half-close	ɪ		ʊ	e, eː ø, øː		o, oː
Half-open	e	ɜː ə	ɔː	ɛ, ɛː œ, œː	ə	ɔ, ɔː
Open	æ	ʌ	ɑː ɒ	a, aː		ɑ, ɑː ɒ, ɒː

This comparison shows that the number of monophthongs in Danish is much greater than that found in English. The situation here is the reverse of that applying to the consonants, where the inventory of the foreign language exceeded that of the mother tongue.

Danish vowel sounds that have no equivalents in English and which the Danish learner should avoid when speaking English, include all the rounded front vowels ([y, y:, ø, ø:, œ, œ:]). Further, the short vowels [i], [u] and [ɑ] (*mit, mut, rat*) are unparalleled in English, and the same applies to the long vowels [e:], [ɛ:], [o:] and [ɒ:] (*mele, mæle, mole, morgen*).

The Danish learner can be expected to have difficulty in pronouncing English vowels that have no counterparts. A case in point is the long, unrounded central vowel [ɜ:], which is non-existent in Danish. Danes tend to replace it by a rounded, half-open front vowel, which they use in English words pronounced with [ɜ:] and spelled with *r*, rendering, e.g., *early* and *sir* as ['œɒli] and [sœɒ] instead of ['ɜ:lɪ] and [sɜ:]. Other examples are English /ʊ/ and /ɔ:/, which are unfamiliar vowel sounds to Danes although in the Danish diagram they correspond to, respectively, /o/ and /ɔ:/. English /ʊ/ is more fronted and considerably closer than Danish /o/, which occurs in words like *kul* and *ost*; and English /ɔ:/ is clearly a more retracted back vowel than Danish /ɔ:/, in, e.g., *måne* and *både*.

The following two word lists compare the English monophthongs with the Danish vowel sounds to which they are most closely related. Attention should be drawn to the fact that few of the word pairs exhibit phonetic identity and that the Danish vowels cited must therefore be modified if they are to be used in English:

English		Danish	
[li:d]	*lead*	['li:ðə]	*lide*
[lɪt]	*lit*	[let]	*lidt*
[let]	*let*	[lɛt]	*let*
[mæd]	*mad*	['ma:ðə]	*made*
[lʌŋ]	*lung*	['lɑŋə]	*lange*
['rɑ:ðə]	*rather*	['rɑ:nə]	*rane*
[wɒt]	*what*	[vɒ]	*vor*
['gɔ:dɪ]	*gaudy*	['gɔ:ðə]	*gåde*
[bʊk]	*book*	[bok]	*buk*
[ru:d]	*rude*	[ru:ðə]	*rude*
['hɜ:njə]	*hernia*	['hœ:nə]	*høne*
['mænəz]	*manners*	['manə]	*mande*

6.5. Vowel length

Above, it was mentioned that English distinguishes between 'long' and 'short' vowels. The first of our two rules that concern vowel quantity deals with this contrast:

A. Given the same phonetic environment, /i:, ɑ:, ɔ:, u:, ɜ:/ and all the diphthongs are longer than the remaining vowels.

The implication of this rule is that /li:d/ (*lead*) and /laɪd/ (*lied*) have longer vowels than /lɪd/ (*lid*) and /led/ (*lead*). Additional examples are /ɔ:/ and /əʊ/ in /kɔ:t/ (*caught*) and /kəʊt/ (*coat*), which are longer than /ɒ/ and /ʌ/ in /kɒt/ (*cot*) and /kʌt/ (*cut*). There is a distinct difference of quantity in these examples: the duration of 'long' vowels has been shown to be almost twice that of 'short' vowels, other things being equal.

When transcribed, 'long' monophthongs are denoted by means of the length symbol /ː/. The digraphic representation of diphthongs may be regarded as an indication of length as well as of two vowel elements. It should be emphasized that 'long' vowels are not always longer than 'short' vowels: a difference of quantity can only be taken for granted in identical circumstances, i.e. when the phonetic environment, the degree of accentuation, the speech rhythm, etc. are exactly the same. If this is not the case, there is much overlap between the two categories.

In our description of the distinction between voiced (lenis) and voiceless (fortis) consonants, we pointed out that the length of a preceding vowel was decisive for the interpretation of a final consonant as voiced or voiceless. In the second of our two rules dealing with vowel length, we shall revert to this phenomenon:

B. All English vowels are relatively short before voiceless obstruents and relatively long before voiced obstruents.

By way of exemplification, it might be mentioned that /ʌ/ is shorter in /bʌt/ (*butt*) than in /bʌd/ (*bud*), that /iː/ is shorter in /liːk/ (*leak*) than in /liːg/ (*league*), and that /aɪ/ is shorter in /aɪs/ (*ice*) than in /aɪz/ (*eyes*). Investigations of these differences of quantity have shown that vowels are only about half as long before voiceless obstruents as before voiced obstruents.

Before final sonorants, i.e. before the class of consonants which are voiced but whose voice has no contrastive function and which may therefore be called neutral with respect to voicing, the duration of vowels is intermediate. The vowel in /bel/ (*bell*) is, e.g., longer than that in /bet/ (*bet*), but shorter than the vowel in /bed/ (*bed*). Similarly, the vowel length in /siːm/ (*seem*) is intermediate in relation to /siːt/ (*seat*) on the one hand and /siːd/ (*seed*) on the other.

If we use the symbol [ː] to indicate full length, [·] to indicate intermediate duration and no symbol to denote considerable shortening, we may illustrate the variations in vowel length discussed above as follows (it should be noted that final vowels exhibit full length):

[siː, siːd, si·l, sit]	*sea, seed, seal, seat*
[bɔː, bɔːd, bɔ·l, bɔt]	*bore, bored, ball, bought*
[praɪː, praɪːz, praɪ·m, praɪs]	*pry, prize, prime, price*
[ləʊː, ləʊːð, ləʊ·n, ləʊθ]	*low, loathe, loan, loath*

The 'short' vowels /ɪ, e, æ, ʌ, ɒ, ʊ/ show corresponding variations in word series such as *bud – bun – but*, *had – hang – hat*, etc., and their relative length may be indicated in a similar manner.

Our two rules governing vowel length often neutralise each other. In the word pair /kɔːt/ (*caught*) – /kɒd/ (*cod*) the 'long' vowel of the first word is shortened before a voiceless obstruent, whereas in the second word no vowel reduction takes place before a voiced obstruent. The joint effect of Rules A and B is that the vowels of *caught – cod* are of approximately identical length. The same applies to word pairs such as /biːt/ (*beat*) – /bɪd/ (*bid*), /hɑːk/ (*hark*) – /hʌg/ (*hug*) and /ʃuːt/ (*shoot*) – /ʃʊd/ (*should*).

6.6. The long monophthongs

Preliminary remarks. In our description of English vowels four items will be taken into account:

1. A description of the *articulation* of the vowel. English vowels being all voiced and oral, the vocal cords will be assumed to vibrate and the velum to be in raised position in all cases.
2. A discussion of the most important *allophonic variants* of the vowel phoneme in question. The length variations to which all vowels are exposed, were accounted for above in § 5.6, § 5.9 and § 6.5 and will not be discussed any further here.
3. A comparison with related vowels in *Danish*; when needed, word lists, etc. will be provided for exercise purposes.
4. An account of *spellings*.

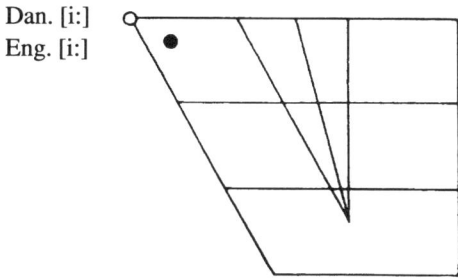

Dan. [iː]
Eng. [iː]

/iː/

(1) *Articulation.* – The front of the tongue is raised in the direction of the hard palate to a height that is slightly more centralised and open than cardinal vowel no. 1. The lips are unrounded. The vowel is articulated with rather strong muscular tension.

(2) *Variation.* – Many English speakers pronounce this vowel as [ɪi], i.e. with a slight front-closing glide, especially in syllable-final position, cf. *be, tea*. There is no need for Danes to imitate this glide, which, when having a central starting point, is non-standard.

(3) *Comparison with Danish.* – Danish [iː] may be transferred to English without being modified.

(4) *Spellings.* – /iː/ is regularly spelled with *ee, ea, e* and *ie*, cf. *meet, flea, secret* and *piece*. Irregular spellings are found in *key, quay, people*.

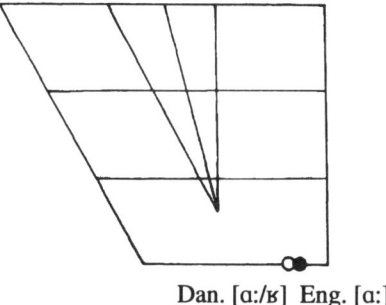

Dan. [ɑ:/ʁ] Eng. [ɑ:]

/ɑ:/

(1) *Articulation.* – The back of the tongue is held in a fully open position, being slightly more fronted than cardinal vowel no. 5. The lips are unrounded.

(2) *Variation.* – There are no important allophones of this phoneme.

(3) *Comparison with Danish.* – The Danish vowel /ɑ:/ that occurs in words like *Maren* and *rase* may be transferred directly to English.

(4) *Spellings.* – /ɑ:/ is rendered orthographically by *ar* and *a*, cf. *hard* and *cask*.

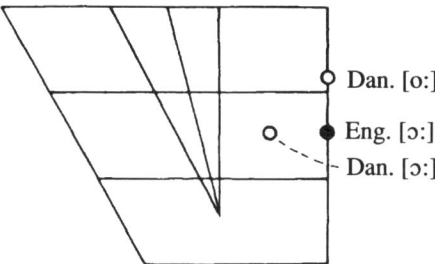

Dan. [o:]
Eng. [ɔ:]
Dan. [ɔ:]

/ɔ:/

(1) *Articulation.* – The back of the tongue is raised in the direction of the velum to a position between half-open and half-close, the quality lying between cardinal vowels nos. 6 and 7. The lips are rounded.

(2) *Variation.* – There are no important allophones of this phoneme.

(3) *Comparison with Danish.* – The vowel attested in, e.g., Danish *nåde* and *håbe* is related to English [ɔ:] and may be transcribed by means of the same symbol. The Danish vowel is somewhat more fronted, however, and may not be transferred to English without modification. The vowel [o:] occurring in, e.g., Danish *kone* is also related to English [ɔ:]; but having a somewhat closer quality, this vowel may not replace the English vowel either. The following word lists compare Danish [ɔ:] and [o:] to English [ɔ:], which qualitatively is something between the two Danish vowels:

Danish /ɔ:/	English /ɔ:/	Danish /o:/
gåde	*gaudy*	*gode*
måde	*Maud*	*mode*
måle	*maul*	*mole*
åle	*all*	*Ole*
låne	*lawn*	*Lone*

The Danish learner may acquire the correct English vowel quality by taking his point of departure in Danish [ɔ:] and retracting his tongue a little in imitation of English [ɔ:]. Once he masters the sound in isolation and in individual words, the learner may go on to practise the pronunciation of English [ɔ:] in longer sequences such as:

I ordered four walkie-talkies from the store.
Alban roared and brandished his sword.
It dawned on Dawson that his daughter was a dawdler.
Paul is an awfully awkward porter.

(4) *Spellings.* – /ɔ:/ is spelled with *au* and *aw*, cf. *audience*, *awful* and with *o* and *oa* followed by *r* as in *or, roar*. Unusual spellings such as *broad, door, floor* and *water* should be noted.

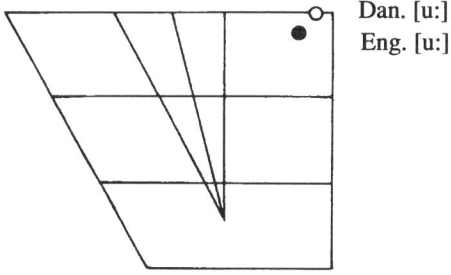

Dan. [u:]
Eng. [u:]

/u:/

(1) *Articulation.* – The back of the tongue is raised in the direction of the velum to a position that is slightly more centralised and open than cardinal vowel no. 8. The lips are rounded. The vowel is articulated with rather strong muscular tension.

(2) *Variation.* – Many English speakers pronounce this vowel as [ʊu], i.e. with a slight back-closing glide, especially in syllable-final position, cf. *do, blue*. There is no need for Danes to imitate this glide, which, when having a central starting point, is non-standard.

When /u:/ is preceded by the palatal consonant /j/, as in *cube* /kju:b/, the vowel is fronted, being realised as a strongly centralised back vowel.

(3) *Comparison with Danish.* – Danish [u:] may be transferred to English without being modified, except after /j/.

(4) *Spellings.* – /u:/ is spelled with *oo*, *o* and *ou*, cf. *fool*, *do* and *group*. Irregular spellings are found in *shoe*, *canoe*, *beauty* and *two*.

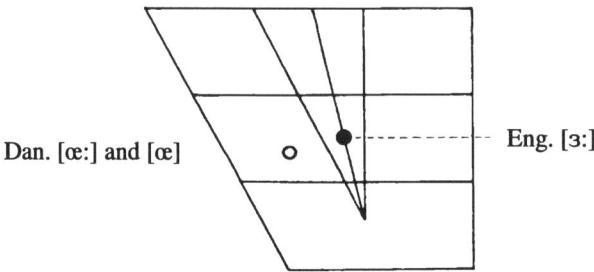

/ɜ:/

(1) *Articulation.* – The centre of the tongue is raised in the direction of the transitional area between the hard palate and the velum to a position between half-open and half-close. The lips are unrounded.

(2) *Variation.* – There are no important allophones of this phoneme.

(3) *Comparison with Danish.* – As pointed out above in § 6.4, Danes are likely to substitute [œɒ] for [ɜ:], but this is clearly an un-English pronunciation. Below, the English monophthong is compared with the Danish diphthong:

English [ɜ:]	Danish [œɒ]
yearn	*hjørne*
first	*først*
her	*hør*
girl	*gør*
thirst	*tørst*
earn	*ørne*

A Danish learner wishing to acquire a correct pronunciation of English [ɜ:], should look upon the vowel as a completely new and unfamiliar type of sound. With narrow opening between the jaws and unrounded lips, he may attempt to imitate the sound as pronounced by English speakers. He should practise the unrounded articulation of the vowel by saying [i: ɜ: i: ɜ: i: ɜ: i: ɜ: ...] without changing his lip position. It is important that the vowel quality remains stable throughout.

The following sentences may be used for practising the pronunciation of [ɜ:]:

> *Have you heard about the earthquake in Turkey?*
> *Irving urged his horse on with his spurs.*
> *They hurled themselves upon the murderer and searched him.*
> *The bird caught an earthworm among the ferns.*
> *Your work is worthless, Mr. Worthing!*

In the last sentence, where [ɜː] follows the rounded consonant [w], unrounded articulation is of particular importance.

(4) *Spellings.* – /ɜː/ occurs only where there is an *r* in the spelling (the only exception to this rule being *colonel*). /ɜː/ is usually spelled *ir, er, ur* and *ear*, cf. *stir, serve, turn* and *yearn*.

6.7. The short monophthongs

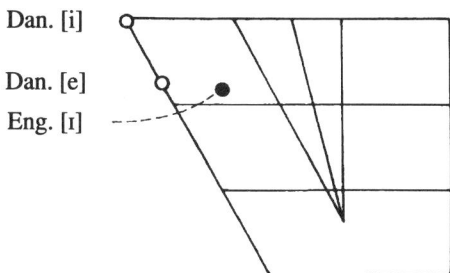

Dan. [i]
Dan. [e]
Eng. [ɪ]

/ɪ/

(1) *Articulation.* – The rear part of the front of the tongue is raised in the direction of the hard palate to a position just above half-close, the vowel quality being that of a centralised cardinal vowel no. 2. The lips are unrounded. The articulation of [ɪ] is lax (unlike that of [iː]).

(2) *Variation.* – In word-final position as in *many* and *heavy*, there is an increasing tendency in English to replace [ɪ] by a somewhat closer sound, not quite as close as the final vowel of Danish *fattig*, but more like a short variety of English [iː]. The first [ɪ] in *city* or *pretty* is thus often less close than the second one.

(3) *Comparison with Danish.* – The accented Danish vowel [e] in words like *midt* and *hedt* is related to English [ɪ]. It cannot be transferred directly to English, however, seeing that [e] is a non-centralised front vowel. In order to acquire the correct [ɪ] quality, the Danish learner should take Danish [e] as his starting point and retract his tongue while keeping it lax. The following word list compares the two vowels:

Danish [e]	English [ɪ]
til	*till*
hedt	*hit*
fedt	*fit*
spille	*spill*

In words like *rich, give, privilege*, which correspond to Danish words with close front vowels (*rig, stiv, give, privilegium*), Danes tend to substitute their short close [i] for [ɪ].

This sounds noticeably un-English, but what is worse, it may also give rise to misunderstanding: [ritʃ] may, e.g., be construed as *reach* (/riːtʃ/) instead of *rich* (/rɪtʃ/) as intended.

The learner may use the following sentences for practising the correct pronunciation:

> *We listened to the pretty hillbilly music.*
> *Finish your dinner, Billy!*
> *It's a pity they killed the pig.*

(4) *Spellings.* – /ɪ/ is regularly spelled with *i* and *y* as in *spirit* and *symbol*. Irregular spellings are found in *busy*, *England*, *lettuce* (/ˈletɪs/), *minute* (noun), *pretty*, *sieve* (/sɪv/) and *women*.

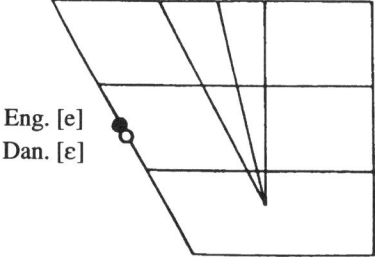

Eng. [e]
Dan. [ɛ]

/e/

(1) *Articulation.* – The front of the tongue is raised in the direction of the hard palate to a position midway between half-open and half-close, the quality lying between cardinal vowels nos. 2 and 3. The lips are unrounded.

(2) *Variation.* – There are no important allophonic variants of this phoneme.

(3) *Comparison with Danish.* – The difference in quality from the Danish vowel [ɛ], which occurs in words like *lægge* and *hest*, is so insignificant that the Danish vowel may be transferred to English. The two vowels are compared in the following word list:

English [e]	Danish [ɛ]
fell	*fælde*
less	*læsse*
vest	*vest*
men	*men*
leg	*lægge*
send	*sendte*

(4) *Spellings.* – /e/ is regularly spelled with *e* and *ea* as in *bet* and *head*. Irregular spellings are found in *any, many, friend, said, says, leisure, bury* and *leopard* (/'lepəd/).

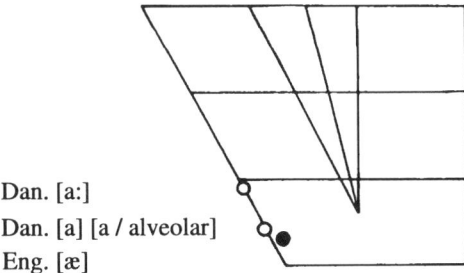

Dan. [aː]
Dan. [a] [a / alveolar]
Eng. [æ]

/æ/

(1) *Articulation.* – The front of the tongue is raised towards the hard palate to a position approximately midway between open and half-open, the quality lying between cardinal vowels nos. 3 and 4. The lips are unrounded.

(2) *Variation.* – Open and retracted variants seem to be increasingly common.

(3) *Comparison with Danish.* – The Danish vowel most closely related to English /æ/ is the short [a] as in *hat* and *kan*. Most speakers of Standard Danish will be able to transfer their Danish sound to English, but it should be noted that there are regional and social variants of [a] which cannot be transferred. The long [aː] in modern Standard Danish is too close to be applicable. Below, a comparison is made between [æ] and short Danish [a]:

English [æ]	Danish [a]
man	*man* (pron.)
tally	*tal* (noun)
mad	*mad* (noun)
had	*had* (noun)
gas	*gas*
plait	*plat*

The following sentences may be used for practice:

> *Hal stabbed his pal in the back with a dagger.*
> *The ambassador left his hat in the taxi-cab.*
> *Alice let the cat out of the bag.*
> *A crash-landing in the valley*
> *The fat man staggered along.*

An important aspect of the acquisition of [æ] is how it relates to [e] and [ɪ], seeing that these three units are distinguished by means of rather slight differences of tongue height:

/ɪ/	/e/	/æ/
bid	bed	bad
hid	head	had
miss	mess	mass
tin	ten	tan
pit	pet	pat

(4) *Spellings.* – /æ/ is regularly spelled with *a* as in *cat* and *man*. Irregular spellings are found in *plait* (/plæt/) and *plaid* (/plæd/).

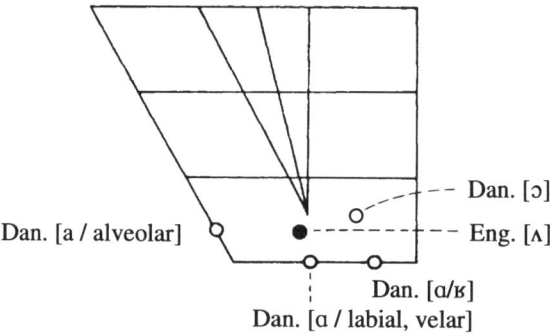

/ʌ/

(1) *Articulation.* – The centre of the tongue moves towards the transitional area between the hard palate and the velum, to just above the fully open position. The lips are unrounded.

(2) *Variation.* – There are no important allophones of this phoneme.

(3) *Comparison with Danish.* – The short Danish vowel [ɑ], which occurs only before labial and velar consonants, after /r/ and in final position (cf. *kaffe, lang, rat, kar* [kɑ]), is phonetically closely related to English /ʌ/ even if it is slightly more open and retracted. In the word list below, the two sounds are compared to each other:

English [ʌ]	Danish [ɑ]
cup	kap
cub	kappe
dumb	damme
cuff	kaffe
tuck	tak
tug	takke
lung	lange

78

Using Danish [ɑ] as their starting point, most speakers of Standard Danish may acquire the correct pronunciation of English [ʌ] by opening their mouths fully and imitating the English vowel. It is difficult for Danes, however, to pronounce the correct vowel quality in front of alveolar and dental consonants, i.e. in positions in which Danish [ɑ] does not occur (cf. English words like *hut, fun, nothing*).

The following sentences may be used for practising the pronunciation of [ʌ]:

> *Mother was run over by a bus.*
> *To conjure up ugly visions of bloodshed*
> *Underdone mutton and boiled onions for supper*
> *He shuddered at the thunder of the guns.*
> *My brother was struck to the ground with an uppercut.*

As we shall see below, the distinction between English /ʌ/ and /ɒ/ presents a serious problem to the Danish learner, whereas he seems to have less trouble in keeping /ʌ/ apart from /æ/:

/æ/	/ʌ/
match	*much*
badge	*budge*
cap	*cup*
lack	*luck*
pat	*putt*
Sam	*sum*

(4) *Spellings.* – /ʌ/ is regularly spelled with *u* as in *hut, sun* and quite frequently with *o* as in *son, honey* or with *ou* as in *country, enough*. Irregular spellings are found in *blood, flood* and *does*.

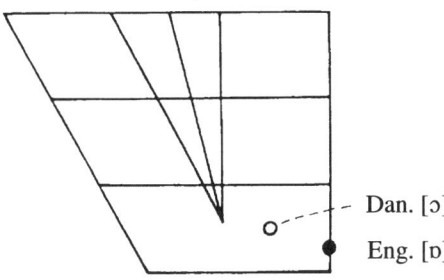

Dan. [ɔ]
Eng. [ɒ]

/ɒ/

(1) *Articulation.* – The back of the tongue is held in an open position that is slightly closer than cardinal vowel no. 5. The lips are rounded.

(2) *Variation.* – There are no important allophones of this phoneme.

(3) *Comparison with Danish.* – In terms of production as well as perception, no phonemic distinction in English causes greater difficulty to Danes than that between /ɒ/ and /ʌ/. They tend to neutralise the vowel contrast, pronouncing for instance *gun* ≠ *gone* alike. Both English [ɒ] and [ʌ] are usually replaced by Danish [ɔ] as in *godt, komme, potte*, and misunderstandings often occur, /ɒ/-words (e.g. *got*) being confused with /ʌ/-words (e.g. *gut*) by the English listener, cf. *Look at the dock* which may be interpreted as *Look at the duck*. It is important to note that English [ɒ] is noticeably more retracted (and slightly more open) than Danish [ɔ], which appears to be closer to [ʌ]. In order to acquire a correct pronunciation of English /ɒ/, the Danish learner should consequently retract the back of his tongue as much as possible in open position. One way to approach the English vowel quality is by using a lowered version of the Danish vowel found in words such as *bort, for, hårdt, kors, kort*. The distinction between English /ʌ/ and /ɒ/ may be practiced by means of examples like the following:

English /ɒ/	English /ʌ/	English /ʌ/	English /ɒ/
shot	*shut*	*cut*	*cot*
lock	*luck*	*fund*	*fond*
donkey	*monkey*	*gun*	*gone*
wrong	*rung*	*cud*	*cod*
don	*done*	*cuff*	*cough*

When the Danish learner is able to identify and produce [ɒ] and [ʌ], he should attempt to distribute the two vowels correctly in the lexicon. This problem can partly be solved by orthographical means in that words spelled with *a* (after *w, u* as in *want, quality*) or *u* create no problems for the learner: /ʌ/ should be paired with *u* and /ɒ/ with *a*. In words spelled with *o*, however, the orthography sheds no light on the distribution of /ʌ/ and /ɒ/, and when this spelling occurs, the correct pronunciation must often be learnt word by word. It is impossible, for instance, to predict that *among, front, month, onion, oven* are pronounced with /ʌ/ and that *cost, got, hob, honour, stock* are pronounced with /ɒ/. The following diagram illustrates the correlation between /ʌ, ɒ/ and the letters *u, o, a*:

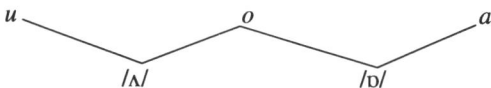

The following sentences may be used for practising the pronunciation of English /ɒ/:

The don was robbed of his wallet.
The robbers were drinking hot chocolate in the lodge.
John got a new stop-watch.

(4) *Spellings.* – /ɒ/ is spelled with *o* and with *a* when this letter is preceded by /w/, as in, respectively, *hot* and *want*. Irregular spellings of /ɒ/ are found in *because, cauliflower, cough, trough, knowledge* and *yacht*.

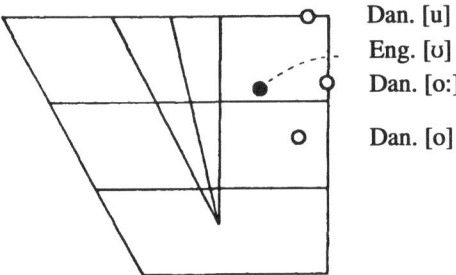

Dan. [u]
Eng. [ʊ]
Dan. [o:]
Dan. [o]

/ʊ/

(1) *Articulation.* – The front part of the back of the tongue is raised in the direction of the velum to a position just above half-close, the quality being a centralised cardinal vowel no. 7. The lips are rounded. The articulation of /ʊ/ is lax (unlike that of /u:/).

(2) *Variation.* – There are no important allophones of this phoneme.

(3) *Comparison with Danish.* – The Danish vowel [o] occurring in, e.g., *ost* and *kul*, is related to English [ʊ]. However, Danish [o] has a somewhat more open quality than [ʊ] and should not be transferred to English without being modified. The two sounds are compared in the following word list:

English [ʊ]	Danish [o]
book	*buk*
look	*lukke*
shook	*suk*

The long Danish [o:] found in *mole, Lone*, etc. also resembles English [ʊ], but since it is more retracted, this vowel quality is not immediately transferable to English either:

English [ʊ]	Danish [o:]
bull	*bolig*
full	*fole*
push	*pose*
good	*gode*

The Danish vowel most closely related is the [o] that occurs in unaccented syllables in for example *topografi, obo, oliere, kopi*. The learner may acquire the appropriate pronunciation of English [ʊ] by taking unaccented Danish [o] as his point of departure and pushing forward his tongue in imitation of the English sound. The vowel in

English words like *foot* and *pull* may be articulated as a centralised (lax) version of the vowel found in the first syllables of Danish words such as *fotografi* and *polere*. An alternative method would be to centralise and shorten Danish [o:], transferring a modified version af the vowel in, e.g., Danish *pote* to English *put*.

In words such as *full* and *put* which have Danish counterparts pronounced with a close back vowel (*fuld, putte*), Danes tend to substitute their short close [u] for [ʊ]. This sounds very un-English and may give rise to misunderstanding: [ful] may, for instance, be perceived as *fool* (/fu:l/) and not as the form intended, viz. *full* (/fʊl/).

The following sequences may be used for practising the pronunciation of English [ʊ]:

> *The butcher stood looking at the bull.*
> *The garden was full of gooseberry bushes.*
> *He understood that his woman was a crook.*
> *You should have a look at this book.*

(4) *Spellings*. – /ʊ/ is spelled with *u* and *oo*, cf. *push* and *took*. Irregular spellings are found in *bosom, wolf, woman* and *Worcester*.

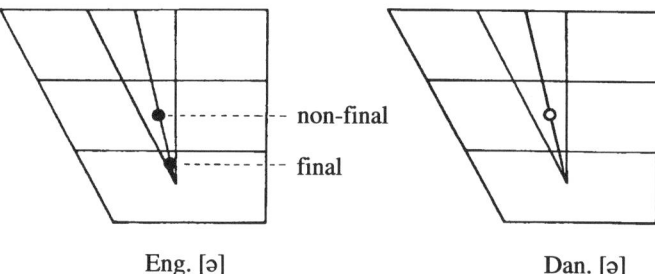

Eng. [ə]   Dan. [ə]

/ə/

(1) *Articulation*. – The centre of the tongue is raised in the direction of the transitional area between the hard palate and the velum to a position between half-open and half-close. The lips are unrounded. Qualitatively, /ə/ is a central vowel that is as far removed from the more distinct, peripheral vowels ([i:, ɑ:, u:], etc.) as possible. It may thus be described as a 'neutral' vowel with the tongue being in its natural position of rest.

(2) *Variation*. – In final position, /ə/ in, e.g., *paper* (/'peɪpə/) is realised as a longer and considerably more open variant than the vowel described above. The [ə] of *sister* (/'sɪstə/) is therefore longer and more open than that of *cistern* (/'sɪstən/).

(3) *Comparison with Danish*. – The [ə] that occurs in Danish *male* (/'mɑ:lə/) and *lægge* (/'lɛgə/) in colloquial speech is identical with non-final English [ə]. The vowel may therefore be transferred to English without modification. The following examples compare Danish [ə] with English non-final [ə]:

English non-final [ə]	Danish [ə]
beggars	*bække*
cistern	*sidste*
colours	*kalde*
western	*veste*
gathered	*gade*

Danish has no vowel corresponding to English final [ə], the final vowel of English *manner* (/'mænə/) being placed about midway between the final vowels of Danish *mande* (/'manə/) and *manna* (/'mana/). A correct pronunciation of this lowered allophone may be achieved by taking Danish [ə] as a starting point and lowering the tongue in imitation of the English sound. The following words may be used for practising the lowered and lengthened pronunciation of [ə]: *actor, borough, brother, caper, centre, china, cover, factor, hover, letter, mother, picture, sister, spanner, villa, winner*.

In acquiring the vowel [ə], it is important that the Danish learner makes it sufficiently short and weakly accented. He may attain such a reduction by for example deleting the [ə]-vowels of *pleasurable, comparable, sufficiency, adversary*, etc. (['pleʒrbl, 'kɒmprbl, 'sfɪʃnsɪ, 'ædvsrɪ]). When he has learnt the correct pronunciation of English [ə], he still has to cope with the problem of using the sound in the appropriate places. No support can be gained from the spellings of words, though it is helpful to know that the vowel is to be found only in weakly accented position. The best way for the learner to get to know the incidence of [ə] in polysyllabic words and connected speech is to use a pronouncing dictionary and to read and write phonetic transcriptions.

(4) *Spellings*. – /ə/ may be spelled with virtually all vowel letters and with vowel letters in combination with -*r* (*forget, brother*, etc.).

6.8. The diphthongs

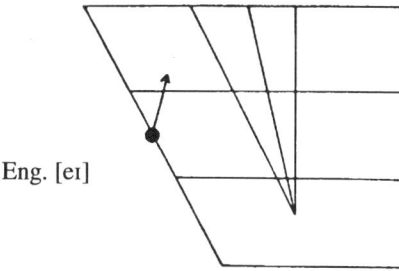

/eɪ/

(1) *Articulation*. – The tongue moves from the position of the monophthong [e] in the direction of [ɪ]. The lips are unrounded.

(2) *Variation.* – The first element of [eɪ] has much latitude for variation between the half-close and half-open positions. This is due to the fact that, with the exception of [aɪ], there are no other diphthongs in the front area with which [eɪ] can be confused.

(3) *Comparison with Danish.* – Danish has no diphthong that is closely related to [eɪ]. Nevertheless, the Danish learner will have no great problem in pronouncing /eɪ/ correctly if he has acquired the English monophthongs [e] and [ɪ]. He will achieve the appropriate sound quality by articulating [ɪ] immediately after [e]: he may for instance take the word *red* ([red]) as his starting point and change it to *raid* ([reɪd]) by inserting an [ɪ].

The following sentences may be used for practising the pronunciation of [eɪ]:

> *Elaine hated railway stations.*
> *They painted the gate yesterday.*
> *Jane failed her examination.*

(4) *Spellings.* – /eɪ/ is regularly spelled with *a*, *ai* and *ay*, cf. *gale*, *mail* and *clay*. Irregular spellings are found in *break*, *great*, *steak*, *gauge* (/geɪdʒ/) and *Gaelic* (/ˈgeɪlɪk/).

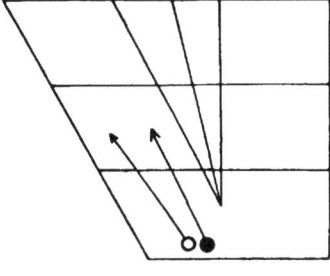

Dan. [ai]   Eng. [aɪ]

/aɪ/

(1) *Articulation.* – The tongue glide begins approximately at the position of the monophthong [ʌ], moving in the direction of [ɪ]. The lips are unrounded.

(2) *Variation.* – The first element of [aɪ] has much latitude for variation in the front and central areas. The considerable degree to which it may be fronted or centralised is due to the fact that [eɪ] and [ɔɪ] are the only other front-closing diphthongs with which [aɪ] can be confused.

(3) *Comparison with Danish.* – Most speakers of Standard Danish pronounce *sejle* and *mejse* with a diphthong which is so similar to English [aɪ] that it may be transferred directly to English. But it should be noted that the social, regional and individual variation characteristic of Danish [ai] is comparable to that of the Danish [a]-monophthongs. In the broad variety of the Copenhagen dialect, the first element is strongly retracted whereas in North Copenhagen it is pronounced as a half-open front vowel; none of these variants are adequate replacements for English [aɪ].

(4) *Spellings*. – /aɪ/ is regularly spelled with *i*, *ie*, and *y*, cf. *mind*, *die*, and *fly*. Irregular spellings are found in *eider*, *(n)either*, *height*, *sleight*, *buy*, *eye*, *guy*, and *choir* (/kwaɪə/).

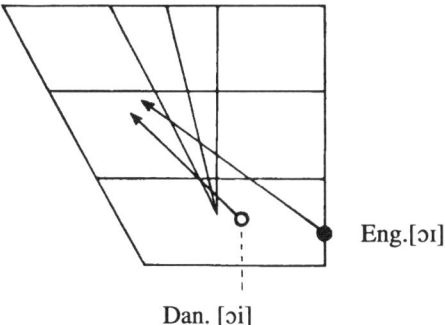

Eng.[ɔɪ]

Dan. [ɔi]

/ɔɪ/

(1) *Articulation*. – The tongue moves from the approximate position of the monophthong [ɒ] in the direction of [ɪ]. The lips are rounded for the first element and spread for the second.

(2) *Variation*. – The first element of /ɔɪ/ has considerable latitude for variation in the half-open and open areas.

(3) *Comparison with Danish*. – In words like *søjle* and *nøgen* Danish exhibits a diphthong [ɔi] which is related to the English sound. Danish [ɔi] diverges from the English diphthong in having a first component which is noticeably more centralised than that of English [ɔɪ]; in addition, the second element is frequently rounded (the pronunciation may be [ɔy]), so the Danish diphthong cannot be used in English unless it is modified. The two diphthongs are compared in the following list of words:

English [ɔɪ]	Danish [ɔi]
boy	*bøje*
coy	*køje*
boil	*bøjle*
loin	*løgne*
soil	*søjle*

If the Danish learner masters the English monophthongs [ɒ] and [ɪ], he should have no difficulty in pronouncing [ɔɪ] correctly. He will achieve the appropriate sound quality by articulating [ɪ] immediately after [ɒ]: he may for instance take the word *con* (/kɒn/) as his starting point and change it to *coin* (/kɔɪn/) by inserting an [ɪ].

The following sentences may be used for practising the pronunciation of [ɔɪ]:

The boy destroyed his toys.
Moira spoiled the oysters by boiling them.
The noise from the adjoining cloister annoyed me.

(4) *Spellings.* – /ɔɪ/ is regularly spelled with *oi* and *oy*, cf. *soil* and *oyster*. Irregular spellings are found in *buoy* (/bɔɪ/) and *buoyant* (/'bɔɪənt/).

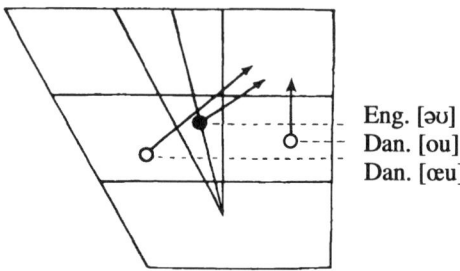

Eng. [əʊ]
Dan. [ou]
Dan. [œu]

/əʊ/

(1) *Articulation.* – The tongue moves from the position of the monophthong [ə] in the direction of [ʊ]. The lips are unrounded for the first element but rounded for the second.

(2) *Variation.* – The first element exhibits considerable variation as regards place of articulation.

(3) *Comparison with Danish.* – Danish words like *snøvle* and *neurose* have a diphthong [œu] which is related to English [əʊ]. The Danish diphthong diverges from the English one by having a rounded and more fronted first element, and it should therefore not be used in English unchanged. The two diphthongs can be compared by means of the following examples:

English [əʊ]	Danish [œu]
hole	*høvle*
stole	*støvle*
sewn	*(i) søvne*
bows	*bøvse*

Another related diphthong which Danish speakers substitute for English [əʊ], is that occurring in *boglig, tåge*, etc. The first component being a rounded back vowel, this Danish diphthong does not qualify for transfer to English either. The Danish learner may acquire the correct pronunciation of [əʊ] by taking English [ɜː] as his starting point and subsequently adding the monophthong [ʊ]. In this way *flirt* (/flɜːt/) may be changed to *float* (/fləʊt/).

The following sentences may be used for practising the pronunciation of [əʊ]:

He moaned over Pope's translation of Homer.
That joker has no soul.
Soames proposed postponing the meeting.
Blow your nose, Jones!

(4) *Spellings.* – /əʊ/ is regularly spelled with *o* and *oa*, cf. *old* and *coal*. Irregular spellings are found in *brooch* (/brəʊtʃ/), *chauvinism* (/'ʃəʊvɪnɪzm/), *mauve* (/məʊv/) and *sew* (/səʊ/).

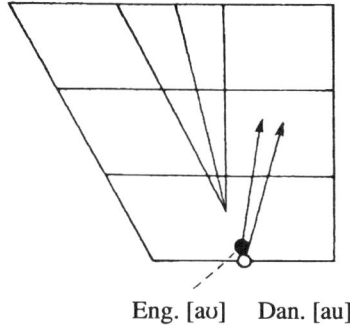

Eng. [aʊ]   Dan. [au]

/aʊ/

(1) *Articulation.* – The tongue moves from approximately the position of the monophthong [ʌ] in the direction of [ʊ]. The lips are unrounded for the first element but rounded for the second.

(2) *Variation.* – The first element of [aʊ] has considerable latitude for variation in the central and back areas. This is due to the fact that, with the exception of [əʊ], there are no other back-closing diphthongs with which [aʊ] can be confused. [aʊ] may have the same central starting point as [aɪ].

(3) *Comparison with Danish.* – The diphthong in Danish words like *navle* and *pause* is virtually identical with English [aʊ] and may therefore be used in English unaltered: the diphthong in *gavne* and *avle* may, for example, be transferred directly to English *gown* and *owl*.

(4) *Spellings.* – /aʊ/ is spelled regularly with *ou* and *ow*, cf. *shout* and *howl*.

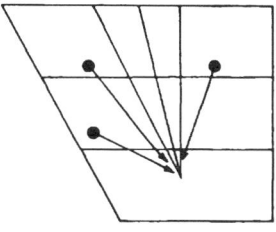   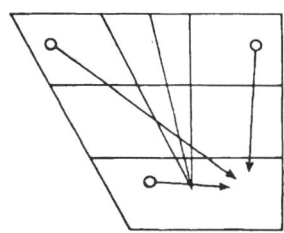

Eng. [ɪə, eə, ʊə] in final position   Dan. [iɒ, ɛɒ, uɒ]

/ɪə/

(1) *Articulation.* – The tongue moves from approximately the position used for the monophthong [ɪ] in the direction of [ə]. The lips are unrounded.

(2) *Variation.* – When /ɪə/ is final as in *fear* (/fɪə/), the quality of the second element is relatively open, being realised almost like the final allophone of the monophthong /ə/.

(3) *Comparison with Danish.* – The Danish diphthong [iɒ], which occurs in for instance the word *kirke*, resembles English [ɪə]. However, the second element of [iɒ] is slightly rounded and more open and retracted, and the first element is closer and more fronted. The two diphthongs are compared by means of the following examples:

English [ɪə]	Danish [iɒ]
fearful	*firben*
pierce	*pirke*
nearness	*nirvana*
beer-house	*birkes*

The Danish learner may acquire the correct pronounciation of [ɪə] by articulating the monophthong [ɪ] immediately followed by [ə] (within the same syllable). Alternatively, he may take Danish [iɒ] as his starting point, lowering and retracting his tongue a little in pronouncing the first element and reducing the tongue glide somewhat.

The following sequences may be used for practising the pronunciation of [ɪə]:

A bearded peer appeared.
The spear pierced Keir's shoulder.
Interference in our sphere of influence

(4) *Spellings.* – /ɪə/ is regularly spelled with *eer* as in *steer* and frequently with *ear* as in *beard*. Irregular spellings are found in *idea*, *real(ly)*, *theatre* and *museum*, where there is no written *r* to parallel /ɪə/.

/eə/

(1) *Articulation.* – The tongue moves from approximately the position of the monophthong [e] in the direction of [ə]. The first element of the diphthong is slightly more centralised and somewhat more open than the monophthong [e], which a comparison between for instance *bed* (/bed/) and *bared* (/beəd/) clearly shows. The lips are unrounded.

(2) *Variation.* – When /eə/ is final as in *there* (/ðeə/), the quality of the second element is relatively open, being realised almost like the final allophone of the monophthong /ə/. The second element being weakened before /r/ as in *vary* (/'veərɪ/), it is difficult to keep, e.g., *Mary* (/'meərɪ/) apart from *merry* (/'merɪ/). There is, however, no overlap in the standard pronunciation of British English between *Mary*/*merry* and *marry* (/'mærɪ/).

(3) *Comparison with Danish.* – The Danish diphthong [eɒ], which occurs in for

instance the word *lærke*, is related to English [eə]. However, the first component in [ɛɒ] is somewhat more open, and the second element is slightly rounded and more open and retracted. The two diphthongs are compared by means of the following examples:

English [eə]	Danish [ɛɒ]
barely	*bærme*
careless	*kærlig*
fairness	*fernis*
scarce	*skærf*

If the Danish learner masters the articulation of English [e], [æ] and [ə], he may acquire a correct pronunciation of [eə] by aiming at something between [e] and [æ], moving his tongue from this starting point in the direction of [ə] (within the same syllable). By way of applying this method, the following examples may be used:

[e]	[eə]	[æ]
bed	*bared*	*bad*
dead	*dared*	*dad*
Ed	*aired*	*add*

Alternatively, the learner may take Danish [ɛɒ] as his starting point, and raise his tongue a little, moving it subsequently in the direction of a neutral central vowel.

The following may be used for practising the pronunciation of [eə]:

Where is the fair-haired girl?
I will leave this bear in your care.
The rare air of the mountains in Eire

(4) *Spellings.* – /eə/ is regularly spelled with *air* as in *flair* and frequently with *are* and *ear* as in *mare* and *pear*. Irregular spellings are found in *scarce, aeroplane, mayor, prayer, vary, wary, Mary, Cary.*

/ʊə/

(1) *Articulation.* – The tongue moves from approximately the position of the monophthong [ʊ] in the direction of [ə]. The lips are rounded for the first element but unrounded for the second.

(2) *Variation.* – When /ʊə/ is final as in *endure* (/ɪn'djʊə/), the quality of the second element is relatively open, being realised almost like the final allophone of /ə/.

(3) *Comparison with Danish.* – The Danish diphthong [uɒ], which occurs in for example the word *urne*, resembles English [ʊə]. However, the first element of [uɒ] is somewhat closer and more retracted, and the second element is slightly rounded and more open and retracted. The two diphthongs are compared by means of the following examples:

English [ʊə]	Danish [uɒ]
bourse	*burde*
moor-cock	*murbrok*
poorly	*purløg*
tournament	*turnering*

The Danish learner may acquire the correct pronunciation of [ʊə] by articulating the monophthong [ʊ] immediately followed by [ə] (without syllabification). Alternatively, he may take Danish [uɒ] as his starting point and lower and centralise his tongue a little, subsequently moving his tongue in the direction of a neutral central vowel.

The following sentences may be used for practising the pronunciation of [ʊə]:

Stuart is a cruel boor.
The judge adjured Muir to tell the truth.
On the moor the tourists ran out of fuel.

(4) *Spellings.* – /ʊə/ is regularly spelled with *ur(e)* and *oor* as in *pure, curious* and *boor* and with *our* in a number of words (*tour, gourd,* etc.). Note *Europe* (/'jʊərəp/), *European* (/jʊərə'piːən/).

(5) *Note.* – Many common words with /ʊə/ have an alternative pronunciation with /ɔː/, e.g. *poor* (/pɔː/), *sure* (/ʃɔː/).

6.9. Vowels in unaccented syllables

The preceding sections dealt with the various English vowels that appear in accented position (as well as with the unaccented unit /ə/). In this section, we will take a look at the vowels in unaccented position. Accent is the topic of Chapter 7, and all that needs to be said here is that English polysyllabic words may distinguish between three degrees of accentuation: main accent, subsidiary accent and no accent. In a word like *photographic*, the third syllable has main accent, the first syllable has subsidiary accent, and the remaining syllables are unaccented.

If we take a look at the unaccented syllables in the words *photographer* (/fə'tɒgrəfə/), *melancholy* (/'melənkəlɪ/), *astonishment* (/ə'stɒnɪʃmənt/), *hopefully* (/'həʊpfʊlɪ/), and in a sentence like *it was a wonderful party* (/ɪt wəz ə 'wʌndəfʊl 'pɑːtɪ/), we find that the vowels occurring there are /ə/, /ɪ/, or /ʊ/. An investigation of a large corpus of words will show that this finding is generalizable: of the English vowels it is the partially centralized units /ɪ/ and /ʊ/ and above all the neutral central vowel /ə/ that are typical of completely unaccented syllables. It is consequently possible to regard these three vowels as reduced forms of the other English vowels; this reduction of unaccented vowels can be illustrated by means of the following diagram, which shows how the monophthongs are weakened:

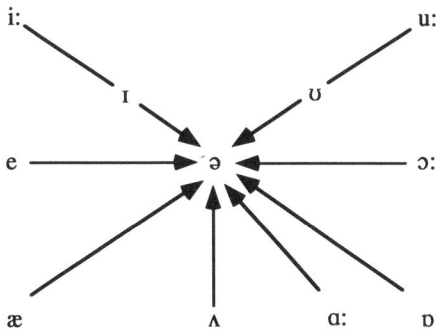

The occurrence of /ə, ɪ, ʊ/ in unaccented syllables is here formulated as a *process*, with e.g. unaccented /ə/ in *atomic* (/ə'tɒmɪk/) being regarded as a weakening of the /æ/ in *atom* (/'ætəm/). This presentation is motivated by a number of vowel alternations which are found in cases of (a) *derivation*, (b) *compounding*, as well as in (c) a class of *monosyllabic words with strong and weak forms*.

(a) Derivations. – A comparison of an English word like *acid* (/'æsɪd/) with the derivative *acidity* (/ə'sɪdətɪ/) shows that the vowel /æ/ in the first syllable is replaced by /ə/ when the main accent is removed from that syllable. Similar weakenings are found with all non-central monophthongs when the accent is lost in derivation:

Accented	Unaccented
/iː/ *regal* /'riːgəl/	/ɪ/ or /ə/ *regalia* /rɪ'geɪljə, rə'geɪljə/
/e/ *recognize* /'rekəgnaɪz/	/ɪ/ or /ə/ *recognizance* /rɪ'kɒgnɪzəns, rə'kɒgnɪzəns/
/æ/ *ally* /'ælaɪ/	/ə/ *alliance* /ə'laɪəns/
/ʌ/ *public* /'pʌblɪk/	/ə/ *publicity* /pə'blɪsətɪ/
/ɑː/ *particle* /'pɑːtɪkl/	/ə/ *particular* /pə'tɪkjʊlə/
/ɒ/ *commerce* /'kɒmɜːs/	/ə/ *commercial* /kə'mɜːʃl/
/ɔː/ *author* /'ɔːθə/	/ə/ *authority* /ə'θɒrətɪ/
/uː/ *tutor* /'tjuːtə/	/ʊ/ or /ə/ *tutorial* /tjʊ'tɔːrɪəl, tjə'tɔːrɪəl/

Although the tendency towards weakening is as described here, it should be noted that in some derivations the unaccented syllable may also have an unreduced vowel on analogy with the vowel in the corresponding accented syllable. Common pronunciations with full vowels are *publicity* (/pʌ'blɪsətɪ/), *authority* (/ɔː'θɒrətɪ/) and *tutorial* (/tjuː'tɔːrɪəl/).

(b) Compounds. – In isolation, the English word *mouth* is pronounced /maʊθ/, but when it loses its accent in a compound, as in *Plymouth* (/'plɪməθ/) and *Portsmouth* (/'pɔːtsməθ/), the vowel /aʊ/ is weakened to /ə/. Similar reductions are found in the following compounds:

	Accented		Unaccented
berry	/ˈberɪ/	strawberry	/ˈstrɔːbərɪ/
board	/bɔːd/	cupboard	/ˈkʌbəd/
land	/lænd/	Finland	/ˈfɪnlənd/
man	/mæn/	milkman	/ˈmɪlkmən/
pan	/pæn/	saucepan	/ˈsɔːspən/
sense	/sens/	nonsense	/ˈnɒnsəns/
shire	/ˈʃaɪə/	Cheshire	/ˈtʃeʃə/
yard	/jɑːd/	vineyard	/ˈvɪnjəd/

(c) Monosyllabic words with strong and weak forms. – In English a number of monosyllabic words have two (or more) pronunciations: a *strong form* with a full vowel, which appears in accented syllables, and a *weak form* (or several weak forms) with a reduced vowel, which occurs in unaccented syllables. This can be exemplified by means of the auxiliary verb *can*. In a sentence like *He can paint*, where the auxiliary is unaccented, we have the weak form /kən/; in the affirmative *He certainly can*, where the auxiliary is accented, we have the strong form /kæn/. The words in question make up a restricted class of words (about 50), short and relatively poor in content, whose frequency makes a correct pronunciation particularly desirable. They can be divided into four subclasses: auxiliary verbs, personal pronouns, prepositions, and a mixed group. (It should be pointed out that not all monosyllabic pronouns, prepositions, etc. have weak forms; normally there is only one pronunciation of e.g. *what* (/wɒt/), *when* (/wen/), *then* (/ðen/), *on* (/ɒn/), *or* (/ɔː/).)

Auxiliary verbs

	Accented	Unaccented
am	/æm/	/əm, m/
are	/ɑː/	/ə/
be	/biː/	/bɪ/
can	/kæn/	/kən/
could	/kʊd/	/kʊd, kəd/
do	/duː/	/dʊ, də/
does	/dʌz/	/dəz/
had	/hæd/	/həd, əd, d/
has	/hæz/	/həz, əz, z, s/
have	/hæv/	/həv, əv, v/
is	/ɪz/	/ɪz, z, s/
must	/mʌst/	/məst, məs/
shall	/ʃæl/	/ʃəl/
should	/ʃʊd/	/ʃʊd, ʃəd/
was	/wɒz/	/wəz/
were	/wɜː/	/wə/
will	/wɪl/	/wɪl, wəl, əl, l/
would	/wʊd/	/wʊd, wəd, əd, d/

The great majority of these weak forms exhibit the reduced vowels /ə/, /ɪ/ or /ʊ/. In the case of *am*, *had*, *has*, *have*, *is*, *will* and *would*, however, we also find weak forms with no vowel at all. These are the cases where the auxiliary is contracted with a preceding personal pronoun, as in *I'm* (/aɪm/), *he'd* (/hi:d/), *she's* (/ʃi:z/), *they've* (/ðeɪv/), *we'll* (/wi:l/), and *you'd* (/ju:d/). (Note that the form *been* may be pronounced /bi:n/ or /bɪn/ whether accented or unaccented.)

Personal pronouns

	Accented	Unaccented
he	/hi:/	/hɪ, ɪ/
her	/hɜ:/	/hə, ə/
me	/mi:/	/mɪ/
she	/ʃi:/	/ʃɪ/
them	/ðem/	/ðəm, əm/
us	/ʌs/	/əs/
we	/wi:/	/wɪ/
you	/ju:/	/jʊ, jə/

Prepositions

	Accented	Unaccented
at	/æt/	/ət/
for	/fɔ:/	/fə/
from	/frɒm/	/frəm/
of	/ɒv/	/əv/
to	/tu:/	/tʊ, tə/

The strong forms are found when the preposition is final in a sentence, as in *What are you thinking of?* (/ɒv/), and frequently when the complement after the preposition is unaccented, as in *She sat staring at him* (/æt/). When prepositions are in their usual position and the complement is accented, the weak forms are normally used, thus e.g. *A bolt from the sky* (/frəm/).

Other words

	Accented	Unaccented
a	/eɪ/	/ə/
an	/æn/	/ən/
and	/ænd/	/ənd, ən/
as	/æz/	/əz/
but	/bʌt/	/bət/
not	/nɒt/	/nt/

some	/sʌm/	/səm/
such	/sʌtʃ/	/sətʃ/
than	/ðæn/	/ðən/
that	/ðæt/	/ðət/ (conj. and rel. pron.)
the	/ði:/	/ðə, ðɪ/
there	/ðeə/	/ðə/ (indef. adv.)
who	/hu:/	/hʊ, ʊ/

This subclass of monosyllabic words comprises conjunctions, pronouns, adverbs and the articles (*a, an, the*). The adverb *not*, the only word exhibiting a weak form without a reduced vowel, is pronounced /nt/ when contracted with a preceding auxiliary verb (*don't, didn't* etc.), otherwise it is pronounced /nɒt/.

It should be emphasized that the weak forms of practically all the words listed above are by far the most common. This is a natural consequence of the relatively low information level of these words. In connected speech the general rule is that words with a high information level (often called *content words* or *lexical words*) are accented, while words with a low information level (called *form words* or *function words*) such as conjunctions, articles, auxiliary verbs, most prepositions and pronouns are unaccented and consequently reduced. The rule may be illustrated by a sentence like *We can hitch-hike to the beach* (/wɪ kən 'hɪtʃhaɪk tə ðə 'bi:tʃ/) with the four short words appearing in their reduced form whereas *hitch-hike* and *beach* have unreduced vowels.

We end this section with a recapitulation. On the basis of the survey of derivations, compounds and monosyllabic words with strong and weak forms, it can be concluded that, as a rule, English vowels in unaccented syllables are weakened to the centralized vowels /ɪ/ and /ʊ/ and, in particular, to the neutral central vowel /ə/. Close front vowels are reduced to /ɪ/, which may, in most cases, be further reduced to /ə/. Similarly, /u:/ is weakened via /ʊ/ to /ə/. All other vowels are reduced to /ə/. Unaccented syllables in English are typically carried by the vowels /ə/, /ɪ/, /ʊ/ or by the sonorants /l/, /m/, /n/ and /ŋ/. The following examples show reduction in an unaccented second syllable: *army* (/'ɑ:mɪ/), *value* (/'væljʊ/), *armour* (/'ɑ:mə/), *battle* (['bætl̩]), *spasm* (['spæzm̩], *cotton* (['kɒtn̩]), and *bacon* (['beɪkŋ̍]).

But this is not a rule without exceptions; in fact, *value* is more commonly pronounced with an unreduced final /u:/. We have also mentioned (cf. § 6.7) the current tendency for the final vowel in *army, city*, etc. to be weakened to a short [i] without being centralized to [ɪ]. In the pronunciation of many younger speakers, examples such as *hopefully, authority, berry* have a close [i] in the final syllable rather than the half-close [ɪ]. This is also true of monosyllabic words like *be, she, the* when unaccented.[1]

---

1. The close pronunciation has become so common that the notation /i/ is used in e.g. Wells 1990 and Jones 1997 to symbolize neutralization between /i:/ and /ɪ/. Similarly, /u/ is used to symbolize neutralization between /u:/ and /ʊ/ in cases like *situation* or unaccented *you*.

Despite this reservation, it is clear that there is a greater tendency to vowel weakening in English than in Danish, cf. word pairs like Danish *mahogni* (/ma-/) – English *mahogany* (/mə-/); Danish *Finland* (/-a-/) – English *Finland* (/-ə-/); and Danish *visdom* (/-ɔ-/) – English *wisdom* (/-ə-/). The correct weakening of vowels in unaccented syllables, normally a source of great difficulty to Danes, is best learned by listening to native speakers, by reading phonetically transcribed texts, and by consulting dictionaries of pronunciation.

7. ENGLISH PROSODY

7.1. Introductory remarks on accent

The preceding two chapters were concerned with the *segmental* part of English phonetics, covering those sound segments (vowels and consonants) which appear in English. A knowledge of that part of phonetics enables us to describe larger linguistic units, such as words and sentences, as being constructed of certain sound segments in a certain ordered sequence. For example, the word *understand* and the sentence *you should have told him,* can be described as the segmental sequences /ʌndəstænd/ and /juʃʊdəvtəʊldɪm/.

A purely segmental description like this, however, is not sufficient. A number of pronunciation features that are characteristic of units larger than the individual segment (syllable, word, word group, sentence) must also be included in a phonetic description. Most important among these is *prosody*, comprising *intonation* and *accent*, which is as central to phonetics as vowels and consonants. Of somewhat less linguistic relevance are the so-called *paralinguistic features*. These are modifications of voice quality, e.g. whisper, tension, huskiness, tremble, which function as indicators of the speaker's attitude to the addressee or to what is said: a happy, disapproving, wondering, conspiratorial, impatient attitude, etc. Non-segmental pronunciation features further include personal voice quality (that which makes a voice recognizable on the telephone) and vocal reflexes like yawning, coughing and sneezing. The non-segmental side of speech production, of which only prosody will be treated here, may be illustrated as follows:

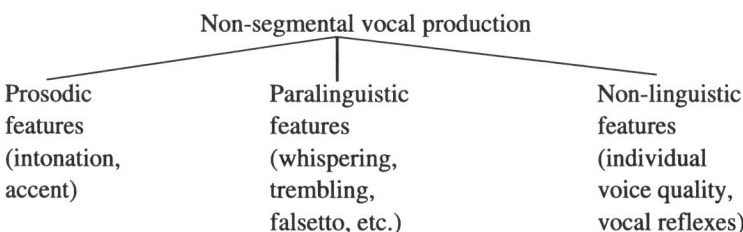

| Prosodic features (intonation, accent) | Paralinguistic features (whispering, trembling, falsetto, etc.) | Non-linguistic features (individual voice quality, vocal reflexes) |

Non-segmental vocal production

In the purely segmental and hence incomplete transcription of *understand* and *you should have told him,* there was no way to capture the relative weight of the syllables. Consequently there was nothing to indicate that the syllables /-stænd/ and /təʊld/ are clearly more prominent than the rest. This relative weight of syllables, however, is as important in the identification of the word and sentence under consideration as are the segmental units, and this is generally true of English polysyllabic words and sentences.

Syllables that are especially prominent are said to be *accented*, and in a transcription they are indicated by means of a preceding accent marker. Accent can be more precisely described as prominence of a syllable in a polysyllabic word or a sentence relative to the other syllables in the same word or sentence irrespective of the phonetic features responsible for this prominence.

Accent in English is produced jointly by four different phonetic factors: stress, tone, vowel length, and vowel quality.

(1) *Stress.* – The term stands for great articulatory energy accompanied by strong expiration. Auditorily stress results in loudness. In a word like *pitiful* (/'pɪtɪfʊl/) the accented first syllable is more strongly stressed and sounds louder than the other two.

(2) *Tone.* – Accented syllables are further distinguished from unaccented ones by means of tone (for the production of voice and pitch, see § 1.2). If a word like *betray* (/bɪ'treɪ/) is pronounced in isolation, the second syllable will become prominent relative to the first because of *tone movement*, i.e. the pitch changes during the articulation of the syllable. In an interlinear tonetic transcription, where the top line indicates the highest and the bottom line the lowest tonal capacity of the voice, and where accented syllables are indicated by big dots, unaccented syllables by small dots, the tone movement can be shown like this:

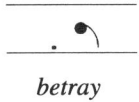

betray

Similarly, in the sentence *you should have told him*, /təʊld/ is made prominent by tone movement:

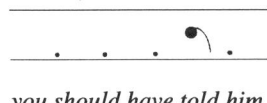

you should have told him

Besides tone movement, the level of the *pitch* as such can contribute to making syllables prominent. This is effected by a shift to another, usually high, level. In a compound like *ice cold*, where both syllables are accented, the prominence of the first syllable is effected by a high tone which stays at the same level:

ice cold

Tonetic prominence may thus be both *dynamic*, as in *(be)tray, told* and *(ice) cold* and *static*, as in *ice (cold)*.

(3) *Vowel length.* – In a comparison of *pharisee* (/'færɪsiː/) with *fallacy* (/'fæləsɪ/) it will be noticed that the last syllable is more prominent in the former word than in the latter. This difference is due mainly to the presence of vowel length in *pharisee* and the absence of it in *fallacy*.

(4) *Vowel quality.* – In a word like *abstemious* (/æb'stiːmjəs/) the first syllable is more prominent than the corresponding syllable in *absorb* (/əb'sɔːb/). This is chiefly

caused by the vowel /æ/ in the first example being distinct whereas the vowel /ə/ in the second example is blurred. A distinct, peripheral vowel quality always gives prominence to syllables in English whereas a blurred, centralized vowel quality – and in the case of syllabic consonants: no vowel quality – does not have this effect.

7.2. The English accentual system

In English, accent often has a *distinctive function*. A comparison of *billow* and *below*, for example, reveals that the two words consist of exactly the same segmental sequence but that the accent in the first word is placed on the first syllable (/'bɪləʊ/) while in the second word it is on the last syllable (/bɪ'ləʊ/). As the two words only differ in a single phonetic feature, position of accent, they constitute a minimal pair. In principle, then, accentual differences can function in the same way as phonemic differences. Occasionally accent has a distinctive function in sentences as well; the sentence *he has plans to leave*, for example, may be pronounced in neutral, unemphatic speech with two different accentual patterns associated with two different meanings:

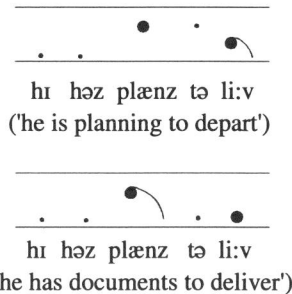

hɪ həz plænz tə liːv
('he is planning to depart')

hɪ həz plænz tə liːv
('he has documents to deliver')

Note that both sentences consist of exactly the same segmental sequence and only differ in that the most accented syllable (with dynamic prominence) is *leave* in the first sentence and *plans* in the second.

Having established that accent in English may have a contrastive function, we must decide how many degrees of accent there are. This is a moot question; our presentation will assume three degrees when words are spoken in isolation (word accent), four degrees in connected speech (sentence accent). The terms used to denote the three degrees of word accent will be main accent, subsidiary accent and no accent, and for these we can list the following phonetic rules of manifestation:

Main accent is associated with *dynamic tonal prominence* (in the form of falling, rising or falling-rising tone movement) and *strong stress*.

Subsidiary accent is associated with *stress*, often with static tonal prominence added.

No accent is characterized by *lack of stress*, most often, though not always, accompanied by the short blurred vowels /ə, ɪ, ʊ/ or the syllabic consonants [l̩, m̩, n̩, ŋ̩].

The occurrence of the three degrees of accent can be illustrated with the following examples:

| ʌnrɪlaɪəbɪlɪtɪ | skuːltiːtʃə |
| kənsɪdəreɪʃn̩ | væljʊəbl̩ |

In these words the syllables /bɪ/, /skuːl/, /reɪ/, /væl/ are pronounced with main accent, the syllables /ʌn/, /laɪ/, /tiːtʃ/, /sɪ/ with subsidiary accent, and the remaining syllables with no accent.

7.3. Accent in polysyllabic words

As mentioned in § 7.2, English has two different types of accent: *word accent* and *sentence accent*. Word accent means that one or more syllables in a polysyllabic word are more prominent than the others when the word is pronounced in isolation. It follows that each polysyllabic word has an inherent accentual pattern. Monosyllabic words, on the other hand, cannot have word accent. Sentence accent means that one or more words in a sentence are made prominent relative to the rest. This implies that monosyllabic words may have sentence accent and that polysyllabic words may be unaccented in sentences. In a sentence starting, for example, *once upon a time ...*, the monosyllabic words *once* and *time* will normally have sentence accent whereas the disyllabic word *upon* will not, the inherent word accent on the second syllable being reduced:

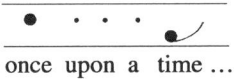

once upon a time ...

The following examples illustrate most possible accentual patterns in English polysyllabic words. (The dashes in the square brackets represent syllables; subsidiary accent has been disregarded.):

Words of two syllables
['- -]   [-'-]
paper   *betray*

Words of three syllables
['- - -]   [-'- -]   [- -'-]
influence *relation* *represent*

Words of four syllables
['- - - -]   [-'- - -]   [- -'- -]   [- - -'-]
melancholy *superfluous* *information* *electioneer*

Words of five syllables

['- - - - -]   [- '- - - -]   [- - '- - -]   [- - - '- -]
spiritually   *administrative*   *aristocracy*   *impressionistic*

As the examples show, virtually all possible accentual patterns are represented; as a consequence word accentuation in English is a fairly complex phenomenon.

As a first approximation to the rules for word accentuation, it may be stated that words of two or three syllables most commonly have the accent on the first syllable, and that longer words most often have the accent on the antepenultimate syllable (the last syllable but two). Examples are *window* (/'wɪndəʊ/), *bachelor* (/'bætʃələ/), *superfluous* (/s(j)ʊ'pɜːfluəs/), *aristocracy* (/ærɪ'stɒkrəsɪ/), *variability* (/veərɪə'bɪlətɪ/). There are so many exceptions to this, though, that it must be said to capture tendencies rather than rules. What follows is a presentation of some of the main rules for word accentuation in English:

(1) *The prefix rule.* – Words of two or more syllables with a prefix usually have the accent on the syllable immediately after the prefix. Examples:

a'rise	*for'get*	*per'sist*
ab'sorb	*fore'see*	*post'pone*
be'guile	*im'pression*	*pre'clude*
com'pose	*in'spect*	*re'semble*
de'tain	*mis'giving*	*sur'round*
dis'grace	*ob'serve*	*trans'plant* (verb)

However, nouns and adjectives often have the accent on the prefix:

'absent	*'discount*	*'misfit*
'concord	*'excellent*	*'permanent*
'context	*'infinite*	*'reference*

(2) *The suffix rule.* – Words with the suffix *-ic* (*-ical, -ically, -icism, -ics*) normally have the accent on the syllable immediately before the suffix. Examples:

ar'chaic	*fa'natically*	*ro'manticism*
characte'ristic	*mathe'matics*	*sta'tistics*
dra'matic	*opti'mistic*	*stra'tegic*
e'lectrical	*pho'netics*	*ter'rific*

Exceptions to this rule are the words *'Arabic, 'catholic, 'heretic, 'lunatic, 'politic(s),* and *'rhetoric*.

(3) *The antepenult rule.* – Words of four syllables or more normally have the accent on the last syllable but two. Examples:

ambi'guity	*elec'tricity*	*pa'renthesis*
a'nalogy	*ha'bitual*	*pho'tography*
bi'ology	*ma'hogany*	*sim'plicity*
co'niferous	*metro'politan*	*spec'tacular*
de'mocracy	*mo'notonous*	*sponta'neity*
di'ameter	*or'thography*	*ther'mometer*

(4) *The word-class rule.* – Word forms with prefix that can represent more than one word class, such as *abstract* (verb, adjective, noun), normally have the accent on the prefix when they are used as nouns or adjectives, but the accent on the syllable after the prefix when they are used as verbs. Examples:

noun/adjective	verb
'addict	ad'dict
'conduct	con'duct
'dictate	dic'tate
'extract	ex'tract
'import	im'port
'increase	in'crease
'insult	in'sult
'object	ob'ject
'permit	per'mit
'protest	pro'test
'suspect	su'spect
'transport	tran'sport

The placing of *subsidiary accent* in English polysyllabic words is chiefly *rhythmically conditioned*. On either side of the syllable with the main accent there is generally an unaccented syllable. Two syllables to the left of the main accent there is normally subsidiary accent, and two syllables to the right of the main accent, likewise, there is most frequently subsidiary accent. This gives rise to regular alternation between accented and unaccented syllables. Symbolizing main accent with (∗), subsidiary accent with (•) and no accent with (°), we can illustrate the alternation with the following examples:

• ° ∗ °	–	*advantageous, information*
° ∗ ° •	–	*enumerate, acclimatize*
° • ° ∗ °	–	*impressionistic, consideration*
• ° ∗ ° •	–	*inexactitude, rehabilitate*

When the subsidiary accent to the left of the main accent is not placed on the expected syllable, the deviation is due either to the presence of an informative prefix, as in *unsystematic* (• ° ° ∗ °), or to analogy, as in *authorization* (• ° ° ∗ °), cf. *author*. Note that in words with two or more syllables to the left of the main accent there is always subsidiary accent on one of these syllables.

In contrast to subsidiary accent early in the word, a subsidiary accent to the right of the main accent is fairly unstable, cf. examples like *influence* (⁍ ○ ○), *melancholy* (⁍ ○ ○ ○), and *spiritually* (⁍ ○ ○ ○ ○).

In words with subsidiary accent to the left of the main accent, the syllable with subsidiary accent may be pronounced with or without static tonal prominence, i.e. at either a high or a low pitch level:

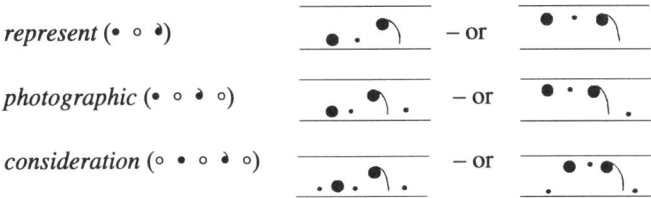

represent (• ○ ⁍)

photographic (• ○ ⁍ ○)

consideration (○ • ○ ⁍ ○)

The pronunciation with static tonal prominence is especially common in long words and in emphatic speech, as in *characterization* (• ○ ○ ○ ⁍ ○) and *idiotic* (• ○ ⁍ ○).

Because of the stable nature of the early subsidiary accent and the possiblility of a high-pitch pronunciation, it is particularly important for Danes to pay attention to it. The following examples may be used for practice:

Subsidiary accent on first syllable	Subsidiary accent on second syllable
characteristic	*accessibility*
circulation	*affiliation*
interdependence	*consideration*
modification	*examination*
reproductive	*impressionistic*
satisfaction	*peculiarity*

The accentual patterns in the words to the left are strongly reminiscent of the patterns in Danish examples like *Inger Merete/frøken Tippe*. In the column to the right the accentuation is close to what is found in Danish sentences like *han spiser flæskesteg/han spiser pølser*. When the words are pronounced with a high-pitch subsidiary accent, they can be parallelled with Danish *gi' mig din taske/gi' mig tasken* (the column to the left) and *hun tog min slikkepind/hun tog min cykel* (the column to the right).

Finally, we need to mention a number of words of two or more syllables which are pronounced in isolation with *subsidiary accent + main accent*. The list includes some words with a prefix, certain geographical names, numerals in *-teen(th)*, as well as a mixed group of words, many of which do not sound entirely English. Here are some examples: *archbishop, unkempt, Chinese, Waterloo, thirteen(th), cashmere, convex, sardine*. In connected speech, words of this type are subject to *rhythmic variation*. When closely followed by an accented syllable – for example when used attributively – they are pronounced with the strongest accent on the first syllable. When this is not the case, the syllable in the second part is pronounced with the strongest accent; and if the words follow an accented syllable closely, their first syllable is given little weight:

First syllable prominent	Second syllable prominent
An unknown master	*He's quite unknown*
The Chinese Wall	*This vase is Chinese*
The fourteenth of July	*July the fourteenth*
Princess Margaret	*A Danish princess*

For words of this type, then, it is the accentual pattern of the sentence as a whole that decides which syllable becomes prominent.

7.4. Accent in compounds

By *compound* we will understand a word consisting of two or more root forms which may also function as independent words. Examples are *airport* and *waste-paper-basket*. In contrast, words like *misfortune* and *breakable*, containing a root combined with a prefix or suffix, and *aerodrome* and *heterogeneous*, consisting of two roots neither of which can appear as an independent word, do not belong to the category of compounds.

In compounds consisting of *two roots,* there are two possible accentuations in English:

1. Main accent on the first element.
   Examples: *dustbin, peanut*

2. Main accent on the second element.
   Examples: *headquarters, ginger-ale*

It is true of both types that in the great majority of cases the element without main accent has subsidiary accent. The accentuation types encountered in English two-element compounds are therefore predominantly main accent + subsidiary accent or subsidiary accent + main accent.

Accentuation Type 1 is the more common. When a compound has become well established and is felt by the native speaker to be a single unit, it will usually be pronounced according to this pattern, i.e. with *unitary accent* on the first element. An extreme example is the word *breakfast* which has become established as a unit to the extent that few native speakers will perceive it as a combination of *break* and *fast* (meaning 'to stop fasting'). The word list below contains some representative instances of nominal and adjectival compounds with main accent on the first element:

airport	*foxhunting*	*school-teacher*
barefoot	*gentleman*	*sight-seeing*
bed-ridden	*gold-digger*	*spitfire*
breakdown	*hold-up*	*steadfast*
come-back	*homesick*	*strait-jacket*
courtyard	*lipstick*	*tea-cup*
craftsman	*make-up*	*typewritten*
dare-devil	*pick-up*	*undertone*
fireside	*playboy*	*waterproof*
flashlight	*rocking-chair*	*wedding-ring*

It is important to note the compounds in this list consisting of verb + adverb (*breakdown, come-back, hold-up, make-up, pick-up*) because Danes can be expected to make the mistake of placing the main accent on the second element on analogy with the corresponding verb group (cf. *That was my steak, Liberty – pick it up!*). Other compounds of this type are *come-down, feed-back, flash-back, hang-over, knock-down, lay-out, pin-up, stand-by*, and *take-off*.

Accentuation Type 2, i.e. where the main accent is on the second element, is found in compounds that are less fully established than the examples listed above with unitary accent. The type may be exemplified by these nominal and adjectival compounds:

blood-red	*fan vaulting*	*lord mayor*
cherry-brandy	*ginger-ale*	*red herring*
coal-black	*guildhall*	*stone-dead*
dog-tired	*home rule*	*working class*

In many cases, such as *front door* and *ice cold*, it is difficult to decide whether we have one compounded word or two words forming a group. The examples given above, though, have enough of a unitary nature to be considered established English words.

Danes usually have difficulty in pronouncing correctly compounds with the main accent on the second element. In Danish there is a greater tendency to unitary accent than in English, and it follows that Danes cannot rely on their intuitions about the accentuation of English compounds. Nor is spelling a safe guide. As a rule compounds written in one word have the main accent on the first element and those written in two words without a hyphen have the accent on the second syllable, but examples like *door handle* (• • ○) and *guildhall* (• •) show that there is no consistency. Moreover, hyphenated spellings abound with both accentuation types. Because Danes have problems with English compounds with the main accent on the second element, we list some more examples of that type:

absent-minded	*mince-pie*
country-house	*prime minister*
downhearted	*public school*
headquarters	*town hall*
lawn-tennis	*weekend*

Note that corresponding Danish compounds like *åndsfraværende, nedslået, hovedkvarter, statsminister, rådhus* and *weekend* are pronounced with unitary accent.

In contrast to compounds with unitary accent, compounds with the main accent on the second element are subject to rhythmic variation in connected speech of the same nature as the simple words with subsidiary accent + main accent (*Chinese, sardine,* etc.) that were mentioned in § 7.3. Examples:

>First element prominent   Second element prominent
>*Absent-minded Joe*   *She's extremely absent-minded*
>*Weekend activities*   *Next weekend*

Compounds with the main accent on the second element may thus occur with a prominent first element, e.g. when used attributively. The picture is further complicated by the fact that some compounds are on their way to becoming well-established units in the language. It is therefore not surprising that some of the compounds listed here under Accentuation Type 2 may also be encountered with the main accent on the first element even if the shift is not brought about by rhythmic variation in connected speech, thus e.g. '*coal-black,* '*guildhall,* '*absent-minded,* '*headquarters,* '*weekend.* There is considerable vacillation, but Accentuation Type 2 exists, and the Danish student must be familiar with it.

Compounds consisting of *three roots* may have the main accent on the first, second or third of these:

>First root prominent
>*aircraft carrier*
>*mother-in-law*
>*merry-go-round*
>
>Second root prominent
>*great grandchild*
>*Never Never Land*
>*picture postcard*
>
>Third root prominent
>*grandfather clock*
>*five-finger exercise*
>*Postmaster General*

In compounds of this type the placing of the main accent is essentially determined by *syntactic* relations. The most common case is that of a two-element compound (pronounced in isolation with unitary accent) which as a whole constitutes an element of a larger compound. This Chinese-box system may be expressed by means of the following diagrams:

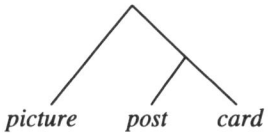
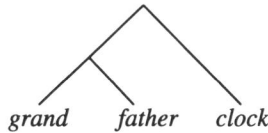

In compounds constructed like this, the accent normally falls on the superordinate element *to the right*, whether this is itself a compound (like *postcard*) or a simple word (like *clock*). Other examples of this syntactically determined accentual pattern are *Irish wolfhound, night-watchman, moving staircase*, where the accent is on the first part of the compounded element to the right, and *blindman's buff, fingertip control, gentleman farmer*, where the accent is on the simple element to the right. The principles for accent placement as presented here cannot, however, be regarded as rules without exceptions since compounds like *aircraft carrier, dirt-track racing, highwayman, holiday-maker, midshipman* are all pronounced with the accent on the first syllable.

Compounds consisting of *more than three roots* are rare. Examples like *jack-in-the-box* and *rag-and-bone man* are pronounced with the main accent on the first and third element respectively.

7.5. Sentence accent and rhythm

In the description of English connected speech, this book operates with one more degree of accent than in the description of polysyllabic words pronounced in isolation. The terms used to denote these four degrees are primary, secondary, tertiary and no accent. The phonetic rules of manifestation are as follows:

Primary accent is associated with *dynamic tonal prominence* and *strong stress*.
Secondary accent is associated with *static tonal prominence* and *stress*.
Tertiary accent is associated with *stress* and *distinct vowel quality and/or length*.
No accent is characterized by the *absence of stress* and most often, though not always, by blurred or lacking vowel quality.

As is apparent, primary accent and no accent in sentences are manifested in the same way as main accent and no accent, respectively, in polysyllabic words pronounced in isolation; an extra degree of accent has resulted from a subdivision of subsidiary accent into secondary and tertiary accent. Schematically the comparison looks like this:

Word accent	Main	Subsidiary		None
Sentence accent	Primary	Secondary	Tertiary	None

The four-level analysis of sentence accent, which will be described more fully in § 7.10, may be illustrated with this example:

You ought to be more co-operative, mister

In this sentence the syllable /ɒp/ is pronounced with primary accent, /ɔ:t/ with secondary accent (static tonal prominence, i.e. prominence brought about by a shift in pitch level), /mɔ:/ and /mɪs/ with tertiary accent, and the remaining syllables with no accent. This makes the following words stand out in the sentence: *co-operative* (strongest), *ought* (second-strongest), *more* and *mister* (somewhat less strong). Note that an interlinear transcription does not directly indicate the difference between secondary and tertiary accent. It is only by checking if a big dot without an attached line deviates from the surroundings with regard to pitch that one can decide whether it represents secondary or tertiary accent. Note also that the first syllable in *mister* has undergone accent reduction by being inserted in this sentence and subordinated to its structure. The inherent accentual pattern of polysyllabic words may be weakened in connected speech, and in that sense word accent is subordinate to sentence accent. On the other hand, where exactly the sentence accent may be placed is dependent on the inherent accentual patterns of the polysyllabic words; in the sentence above, for example, the sentence accent falls on the second syllable of *co-operative*, and that is the only possibility in this polysyllabic word. Word accent and sentence accent in English are thus mutually dependent patterns.

In sentences and connected speech the most important words are regularly accented, and sentence accent is thus *semantically conditioned*. In our sentence above, for example, the words *co-operative* and *ought* have primary and secondary accent, respectively, because they are most important in content, and *more* and *mister* have tertiary accent because they are more informative than the remaining words. A further example is this sentence:

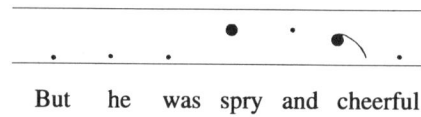

But he was spry and cheerful

Here *spry* and *cheerful* are the most informative words and hence phonetically prominent, whereas the remaining words are less important and consequently unaccented.

In § 6.9, where strong and weak forms were discussed, it was pointed out that so-called form words, i.e. relatively uninformative words like auxiliary verbs, prepositions, articles, conjunctions, and many pronouns, are generally unaccented in connected speech, whereas so-called content words, like nouns, adjectives, many adverbs, and most main verbs, are accented. This is the case in the two examples above, as well as in the following sentences:

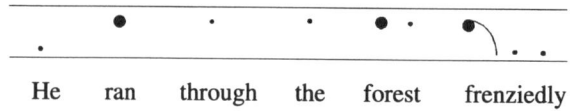

He ran through the forest frenziedly

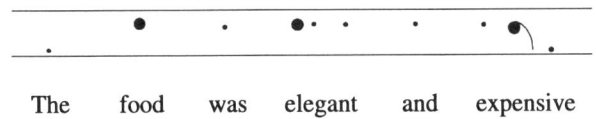

The food was elegant and expensive

Because of their characteristic linguistic function, then, some words, e.g. *the* and *and*, are predisposed to be unaccented in connected speech, others, e.g. *elegant* and *frenziedly*, to be accented.

In English there is a tendency towards a certain type of *sentence rhythm*. It is brought about by the syllables with sentence accent (primary, secondary, tertiary) being approximately isochronous, i.e. separated by time intervals of roughly the same size. This phenomenon can be illustrated with the following examples:

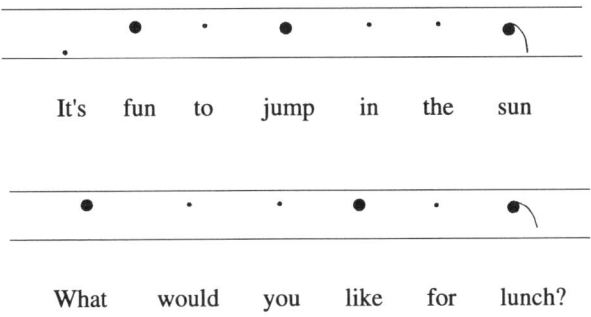

It's fun to jump in the sun

What would you like for lunch?

If you read these sentences aloud in a natural manner and tap your desk when you pronounce an accented syllable (*fun, jump, sun / what, like, lunch*), you will produce a rhythmic pattern. If you tap each time you pronounce a syllable, the result is clearly arhythmic.

The accented syllables of English sentences tend to be isochronous whether they are separated by many or few unaccented syllables. The result is that the speed of articulation is accelerated when there are many unaccented syllables between the accents, and is retarded when there are few unaccented syllables. The duration of the unaccented syllables is thus inversely proportional to their number. If there are no unaccented syllables at all between the accented syllables of a sentence, the speed of articulation will be strongly reduced. This is illustrated in the following examples where the pattern of approximately equal time intervals between the accented syllables is reflected in equal spacing of the printed line:

Wasn't it	*last*	*Monday?*
But wouldn't it be	*perfectly*	*sweet of her?*
John	*won't*	*sleep*

Languages with a tendency to isochronous accents, such as English and Russian, are said to have *accent-timed rhythm*. In a number of other languages, e.g. French and

Spanish, the sentence rhythm is the result of a tendency for the syllables, both accented and unaccented, to be isochronous; such languages are said to have *syllable-timed rhythm*. As impressionistic synonyms for the terms syllable-timed and accent-timed rhythm one may use *machine-gun rhythm* and *morse rhythm*.

Like English, Danish has accent-timed rhythm, so one would not expect the characteristic acceleration and retardation of the speed of articulation in English sentences to be a major obstacle for Danes. Nevertheless, sentences with strongly accelerated speed do cause problems for Danes because the articulation is not fully automatized as is the case with sound sequences in the native language. If this problem is to be solved, it is a good idea to divide sentences into rhythmic groups and pronounce each group as if it were a polysyllabic word. For example, the sentence *But wouldn't it be perfectly sweet of her?* can be divided into the rhythmic groups *But wouldn't it be – perfectly – sweet of her*; the first and last group can then be spoken with the rhythm of polysyllabic words of the type *administrative* and *bachelor*. After a fluent and rapid pronunciation of each group has been mastered, the learner must try to link the groups together and pronounce the entire sentence in one uninterrupted articulatory movement.

We have described the accent-timed rhythm of English as a *tendency*, and we must emphasize that it is far from the rigour of a metronome. It is also an unsettled matter to what extent syllables with tertiary accent carry the rhythm of the sentence. If the syllable /re/ in a sentence like *It's a representative collection* is pronounced with tertiary accent, the speed of articulation seems to become somewhat retarded, though less so than if the syllable is pronounced with secondary accent (cf. § 7.3 on the subsidiary accent in words like *represent*):

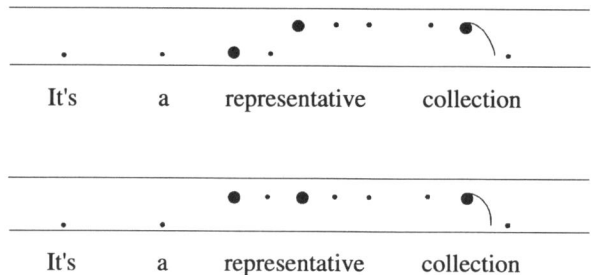

7.6. Introductory remarks on intonation

By 'intonation' we will understand that part of the pronunciation of a language which is tonal in nature, i.e. phenomena like pitch level, pitch range and tone movement. Intonation is closely connected with accent, and in English it is not possible to keep intonation completely separate from accent and related prosodic phenomena like rhythm and speed of utterance. As mentioned in § 7.1, the intonation of sentences is depicted in an interlinear transcription system, i.e. an adapted form of musical notation where the upper and lower lines represent the limits of a speaker's normal range of voice, and where the position of the dots – small ones for unaccented syllables, big ones for accented syllables, and big ones with a line attached for accented syllables with tone movement – corresponds to their relative pitch. To some extent this type of transcription has already been used in the preceding sections on accent. It can be further illustrated by means of the following example which shows, among other things, how the first two words are pronounced at a fairly low pitch level; that there is then an upward jump on the first accented syllable; and that the last word of the utterance is pronounced with a strong downward tone glide.

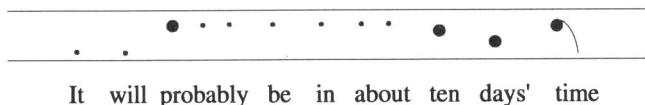

It will probably be in about ten days' time

In contrast to musical notation, the interlinear transcription only holds information about the *relative* pitch of the syllables. The fixed intervals and absolute pitch of music are not found in normal speech, only in very special situations, such as in calling someone's name or in certain forms of children's language:

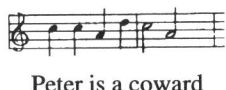

Peter is a coward

In certain languages – the so-called *tone languages*, spoken mainly in the Far East, in Africa, and by some American Indians – tone is an integral part of the individual word and contributes to its lexical meaning on a par with the segments. In Thai, for example, *maa* means 'horse' when spoken with a high tone, 'come' when spoken with a mid tone, and 'dog' when spoken with a rising tone. Word tones are also found in Norwegian and Swedish although to a limited extent. For example, in (some varieties of) Norwegian the pronunciations of *bønder* ('peasants') and *bønner* ('beans') are only kept apart by the former being said with a rising tone (called Tune 1) and the latter with a composite falling-rising tone (Tune 2). In languages where tone does *not* have a lexical function, among them both English and Danish, tone is not attached to the word but to larger syntactic units such as word groups and clauses. The intonation with which such units are spoken expresses meanings that serve primarily to indicate attitude. The following example will illustrate this:

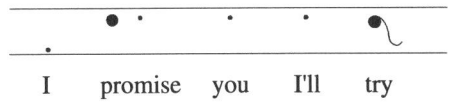

I promise you I'll try

In pronouncing this sentence with an intonation contour as indicated (i.e. with falling-rising tone on the last syllable), the speaker adds to its meaning an element of reservation or doubt as to the projected outcome of the action promised; the content of the utterance is changed but without altering the individual words. Similarly, the intonation used in the pronunciation of /ə 'dɒg/ says something about the speaker's attitude, e.g. degree of interest, but the sound sequence refers (in contrast to Thai *maa*) to the familiar domestic quadruped whether said with a high or low, rising or falling tone.

Intonation does not vary freely or in an unprincipled manner; it is *systematic* and *conventional*. The speaker employs a limited number of patterns learned in childhood and used to achieve certain effects. Intonation is also *language-specific*, so English intonation differs from that found in any other language, including Danish. It follows that the patterns which a speaker of another language automatically transfers from his mother tongue to English are generally wrong and may lead to misunderstanding or irritation. If, for example, a Dane is in a situation that demands an unqualified apology and reacts by saying *I'm sorry* with a very narrow pitch range – and that is to be expected – it could be interpreted as lack of a genuine sense of guilt. For in English a sincere apology is said with a relatively wide pitch range, in this case usually in the shape of a forceful falling-rising tone movement on the adjective.

It was mentioned above that intonation expresses meanings that primarily indicate attitude, and we shall now take a closer look at the main functions of intonation in English. Occasionally intonation has a *grammatical function*, i.e. it is used to express clear-cut differences of meaning similar to those commonly signalled syntactically:

You've got a cold   You've got a cold?

The difference between a statement and a question that demands yes or no as an answer – a difference normally signalled by the presence/absence of inversion or *do-*support – is here expressed exclusively by means of two different intonational patterns. This grammatical role of intonation is rather limited in English, though, and often intonation has a purely *attitudinal function*. A sentence like *What are you knitting?*, for example, can be said with two different intonation contours, and in this case exchanging one for the other results in a relatively insignificant change of meaning: with falling intonation the request for information is quite neutral; with rising intonation there is an added indication of polite interest and possibly diffidence ('May I ask?').

Besides having grammatical and attitudinal functions, intonation in English contributes decisively to the *segmentation of speech*. By listening carefully to connected speech you will discover that it is organized as acoustically signalled *units of information*. This organization can be illustrated with the following example where the boundaries between units are symbolized by vertical lines:

> I don't think, you see | that any progressive government | a Labour government | could possibly have done it | and the reason for that is | that we would have been sniped at | consistently | by the Conservative Party | in the House of Commons.

This division into units or blocks, without which the listener would find it difficult to understand the message, is only to a small extent signalled by regular pauses. In the authentic example above, the speaker only paused to breathe before *and*. Of much greater importance for the segmentation of speech is the intonation contour. Each unit of information is spoken with one integrated contour centring around a syllable pronounced with primary accent, i.e. with a *tone glide* (in this case around *think*, *(pro)gress(ive)*, *La(bour)*, *done*, the demonstrative *that*, *sniped*, *(con)sist(ently)*, *(Con)ser(vative)*, and *Com(mons)*). For this reason the blocks of information that connected speech is divided into, are called *tone groups*. Organization into tone groups – the detailed description of which we shall return to in the next section – is to some extent determined by syntactic structure. But the tone group does not correlate with one specific syntactic unit (such as the clause). In the example above – a complex sentence consisting of two parallel clauses co-ordinated by *and* – the tone groups correspond to syntactic constituents of several types.

7.7. The tone group

We shall begin by defining the tone group as *a section of speech containing one peak of prominence in the form of a syllable pronounced with tone glide and strong stress* (i.e. with primary accent). This definition does not enable us to determine the boundaries of the tone group, but we shall return below to the question of criteria for demarcation. The organization of speech into tone groups can be illustrated with the following example where the syllables *tour-*, *-tend*, and *-ta-* constitute the peaks of prominence:

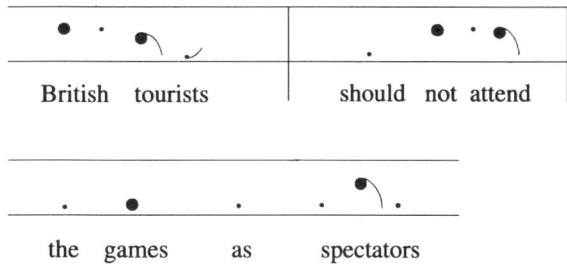

The peak of prominence is referred to as the *nucleus* of the tone group, and the nucleus is the only obligatory part of the tone group. The maximum number of components in the tone group is four: nucleus, head, springboard, and tail. By the *head* of the tone group we understand the section of speech stretching from the first syllable pronounced with secondary accent (i.e. with stress and static tonal prominence, cf. § 7.5) to the nucleus. By *springboard* is meant the section of speech stretching from the beginning of the tone group to the head, or – if there is no head – to the nucleus. Finally, *tail* refers to the section of speech stretching from the nucleus to the end of the tone group. The internal structure of the English tone group can be expressed by the formula (S) (H) N (T), where the letters symbolize 'springboard', 'head', 'nucleus', 'tail', and where the optional components are in parentheses. We can illustrate this structure with the same example as was used in § 7.6:

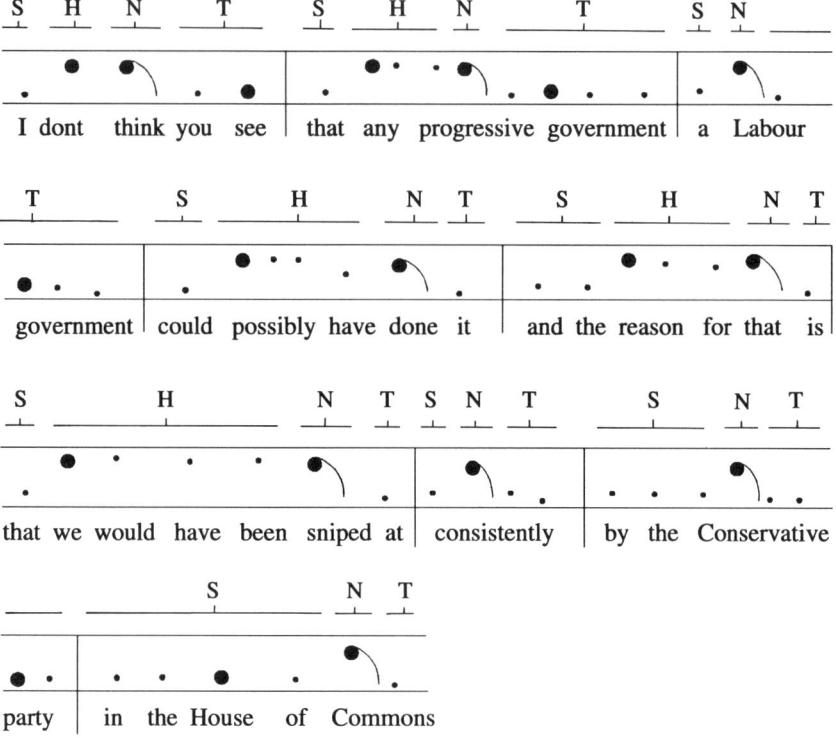

As mentioned, springboard, head and tail are not obligatory parts of the tone group. In this example four of the tone groups do not have a head; in *British tourists* and *should not attend* (in the preceding example) there is no springboard and tail, respectively; and a tone group carried by the word *well*, for example, will have neither springboard nor head nor tail.

Tone-group boundaries are signalled in several ways:

(1) By a *change of pitch*, either in the form of an upward jump (after tone groups ending in a fall) or a downward jump (after tone groups ending in a rise). These shifts in pitch level, which can also be observed in the examples above, are due to the fact that tone groups with a springboard begin on one and the same 'neutral' pitch level, more precisely at the lower edge of the mid level.

(2) By a *prolongation* of the nucleus and any following tail. That is to say, the speed of utterance is slowed down towards the end of a tone group.

(3) Sometimes by a *pause* (allowing the speaker to breathe).

On the basis of the tone-group definition and the particulars about tone-group boundaries given above, attentive and repeated listening to tape recordings should enable the student to break down connected speech into tone groups.

The *springboard* of the tone group has its name because it is normally at a low level from which the transition to the head (or nucleus) may be envisaged as a jumper's take-off. The *head* of the tone group is normally spoken either at a high level over its entire duration or with a gradually falling intonation after a high beginning. These two varieties can be illustrated with the following examples, where it is important to note that the unaccented syllables of the head are at the same pitch level as the immediately preceding accented syllable:

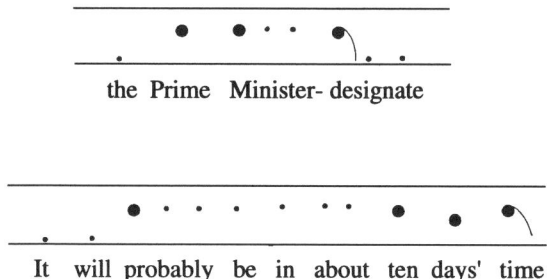

Occasionally an *upward tone jump* occurs on a non-initial syllable in the head of the tone group. Such an upward jump, resulting in secondary accent, takes place on and serves to emphasize a word that is important in the context:

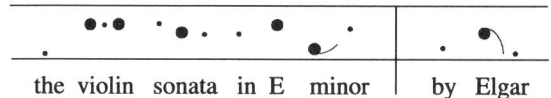

The *nucleus* is the part of the tone group which is *most important in content*. Its function is to express what the speaker chooses to make the main point of his message. In the following example, where the words that make up or contain a nucleus are in italics, the portions of the message thus marked are to be regarded as its key words:

> *But* | in *answer* | to the *question* | that was *put* | I mean what do the *Conservatives* | think of the *result* | *I* | would have *thought* | that the Conservatives were *so* | *delighted* | to have got off the *hook* | that they really didn't care *what* the result was going to be.

Finally it should be mentioned that the nucleus is most often *placed on the last content word* in a tone group (cf. § 6.9 and § 7.5 about content words and form words). This position of the nucleus can be observed in most of the tone groups in the example above. Sometimes, though, the nucleus is carried by a form word (*but*, *I*, etc.). And in many cases the nucleus is *not* manifested by the last word but by an earlier word in the tone group (normally a content word). This *nucleus advancing* turns a non-final word into the peak of prominence in the tone group with the result that it stands out. An advanced nucleus is found in the last tone group in the example above (setting off the word *what*). That meaning may be drastically affected is abundantly clear from the following examples:

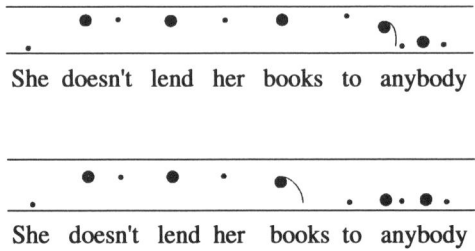

The bottom sentence, which differs from the top sentence by nucleus placement, implies that while the person in question does not lend her books, she is probably willing to lend other belongings.

7.8. The classification of tone groups

English tone groups can be divided into three different types on the basis of the tone movement that takes place in the nucleus and a following tail (if any): *falling*, *rising*, and *falling-rising*. The three types are not equally common. According to Crystal (1969:225), a little over half of all tone groups in conversational English are falling. Second in frequency is the rising type, but the falling-rising is almost as common. As the following examples demonstrate, the three tone-group types are all distinctive as to meaning:

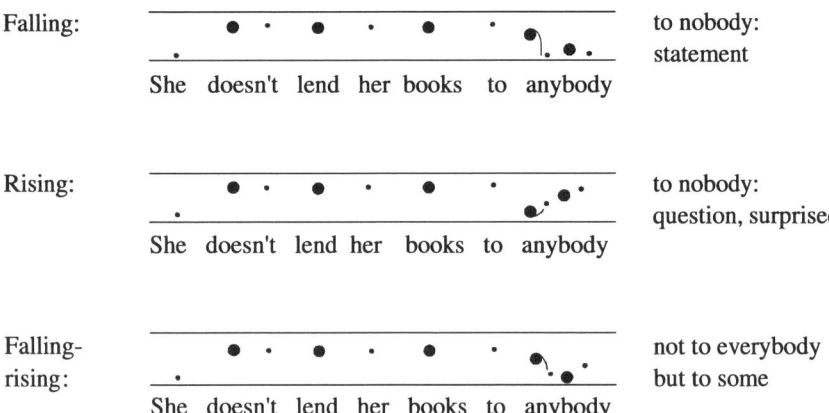

The general meaning and use of the tone-group types may be explained on the basis of the following three contrasting pairs: *certainty/uncertainty as to yes or no*, *kindness/unkindness*, and *completeness/incompleteness*.

Concerning the first of these pairs, it can be said that as a rule the speaker will use a rising tone group when she does not know whether the state of affairs that her utterance refers to is positive or negative, i.e. in the so-called yes-no questions, such as *Is that all, dear?* The falling tone group, on the other hand, signals that there is no uncertainty as regards positive-negative; it will be used in utterances like *It doesn't really count* and *What would you like for lunch?* The complex falling-rising tone group may be said to reflect a complexity of content as it combines certainty with an element of doubt. By the falling glide (or 'down-glide') the speaker shows that she knows if the state of affairs referred to is positive or negative, but by the following rise she further indicates that there is more to say about it:

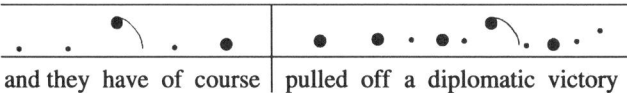

and they have of course	pulled off a diplomatic victory

The falling-rising pattern of the second tone group here signals that while the state of affairs is positive (+ diplomatic victory), a *reservation* is also expressed, i.e. there is a latent 'but' in the utterance. In the case in question we can make this reservation explicit by quoting the next tone groups: *but in the end | it doesn't really count | whether the Conservative Party | or whether the British are pleased.*

The second contrasting pair has been proposed because a connection can be observed in English between kindness and rising or falling-rising tone groups on the one hand, and between unkindness and falling tone groups on the other. In some types of utterance the (falling-)rising contour expresses an obliging, polite, perhaps cautious attitude, while the falling contour is used when there is no wish to signal such an attitude. We can illustrate this with an example like *What are you knitting?* (discussed in § 7.6). In other types of utterance a falling tone indicates unkindness and the like, whereas the rising and falling-rising tone group types do not create that impression. If, for example, the first tone group in an alternative question like *Would you like coffee | or tea?* is spoken with a falling pattern, this will indicate unfriendliness or at least impatience. If spoken with a rising or falling-rising contour, however, the effect is neutral.

Finally there is a certain connection between incompleteness and the (falling-)rising tone-group types, and between completeness and the falling type. In the following example the final tone group is spoken with falling tone, indicating completeness, and two of the non-final groups with a (falling-)rising pattern, indicating incompleteness:

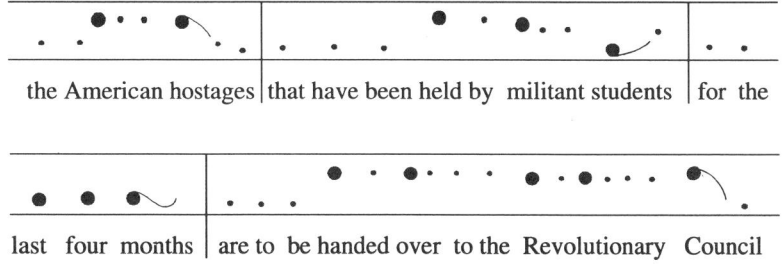

the American hostages	that have been held by militant students	for the

last four months	are to be handed over to the Revolutionary Council

While the correlation between completeness and falling contour is fairly stable, the correspondence between incompleteness and rising/falling-rising contours is far from mechanical. That we can only talk about a tendency emerges particularly clearly from the second example in § 7.7, where a string of non-final tone groups are spoken with a falling contour.

The three tone-group types can be realized with a wider or narrower *pitch range*, and this affects their meaning considerably. The following dialogue is a clear example of pitch range being semantically relevant:

A: Some tea?   B: Some tea?!

Here A asks B if he wants tea, using for this purpose a moderate pitch range. To B, however, the situation appears to be such that drinking tea would be an unreasonable activity. So he answers with a surprised 'echo question' or 'question to the second power') which he pronounces with a wide range, and which may be paraphrased 'Did I understand? Do you really mean...', etc. In falling and falling-rising tone groups an increase in pitch range has the same intensifying effect. While an increase intensifies, a narrowing of pitch range has a weakening effect.

Finally it should be pointed out that in this book we use the following convention when transcribing falling-rising tone groups containing a tail:
    (1) If there are one or more accented syllables in the tail and the last syllable of the tail is unaccented, there is a *stepping rise* from the last accented syllable of the tone group. Examples:

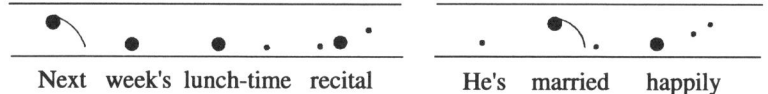

Next week's lunch-time recital   He's married happily

(2) In all other cases there is a *rising glide* (or 'up-glide') on the last syllable of the tail. Examples:

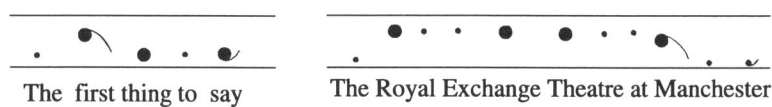

The first thing to say   The Royal Exchange Theatre at Manchester

7.9. Comparison with Danish

In Chapter 3 it was mentioned that students of a foreign language tend to replace unfamiliar features with those most closely related in the mother tongue. This propensity to substitution can be observed not only at the segmental level but also within prosody. To a large extent Danish students will transfer the tonal pattern of their mother tongue to English, and as English and Danish patterns differ in essential points, the consequences are unfortunate. As mentioned in § 7.6 above, one of the main functions of intonation is to convey attitudes, so it stands to reason that a transfer of deviant, Danish patterns to English may result in misunderstanding of the speaker's attitude towards both the listener and the circumstances that an utterance refers to. Since intonation probably represents the most unconscious and ingrained part of the pronunciation of a language, the difficulties in ridding oneself of rules stemming from the mother tongue are greater here than in any other area of pronunciation. This state of affairs is reflected in the fact that many Danes who have acquired a good English pronunciation at the segmental level, nevertheless speak English with Danish intonation. This lopsidedness is not unproblematical. For one thing the transfer of Danish intonation, as we said, results in other attitudes being signalled than those intended or appropriate in a given situation. It has been said that a Swede who uses the intonation of his mother tongue in English will sound 'amiably imbecile, like a stupid aunt talking to a young child'. When Danish intonation – whose main features will be described below – is transferred to English, it will often give English-speaking people an impression of dejectedness, disinterest or apathy, attitudes which will be out of place in most situations. In addition, intonational errors may be more offensive than other errors in pronunciation. If a Dane has an otherwise acceptable pronunciation of English, the English listener will tend to assume that a given tonal pattern – transferred from Danish – is not simply a foreigner's error but that it is consciously employed to express a certain attitude. As a result speakers of English will often find it more difficult to accept intonational errors than other errors of pronunciation.

It goes without saying that in the process of acquiring the intonation of English, students should use their imitative abilities to the full, but there is no doubt that a conscious and analytical method of learning will in most cases lead to the best results. This is expressed by O'Connor & Arnold (1973:98) as follows:

> there are some gifted people who can acquire the tunes of English by simply imitating what they hear around them, but most foreign students cannot do this and would be unwise to think they can.

The most efficient learning strategy is to become conscious of the main differences between English and Danish intonation, and then work selectively with the aspects that are most unfamiliar. It should be added that the learning problems are not only of a linguistic and musical nature but also to a large extent psychological. The typically English intonation – characterized in particular by a wide range, high-level heads and strong glides – strikes Danes, except in emphatic speech, as being exaggerated and histrionic. Consequently Danes will feel that they themselves sound insincere, affected and somewhat hysterical when they imitate English intonation. It is, however, important to remember that the tonal patterns employed do *not* give speakers of English an impression of attitudes of that sort.

When Danes have learned to reproduce the intonation of English utterances in a teaching situation – e.g. in a language laboratory – they normally have a hard time trying to transfer this skill to spontaneous conversation. The solution to this difficult problem must be to work with characteristic English intonation contours until they become *automatized*, cf. again O'Connor & Arnold (1973:98):

> There is only one way to master the pronunciation of a foreign language: to repeat the sound features of the language over and over again ... until they can be said without any conscious thought at all, until the learner is incapable of saying them in any other way.

After these general considerations, let us point out some major features of the Danish system of intonation and in that way isolate the tonal areas of English that present special problems for Danes. One of the most striking characteristics of (East) Danish intonation is the *relation between accented and unaccented syllables*: an unaccented syllable is usually spoken at a higher pitch than the immediately preceding one; and if there are several unaccented syllables between two accented ones, they are pronounced with a falling tone movement (cf. Thorsen 1978). This results in a *weaving pattern* which can be illustrated with the following examples:

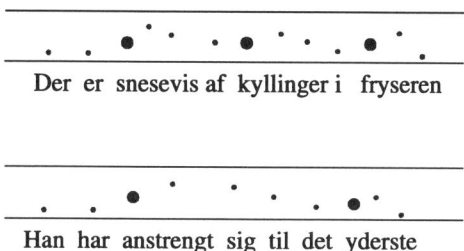

Because of this weaving tonal contour of the mother tongue, Danes have problems with the *head of the tone group* in English. As mentioned in § 7.7, the head of an English tone group is spoken at a high pitch over its entire duration or with gradually falling pitch, but regardless whether one or the other of these varieties is used, the unaccented syllables of the head are at the *same pitch level* as the accented syllable that precedes them. As weaving heads of the type mentioned are unknown in English, it is important that Danes rid themselves of this aspect of the intonation of their mother tongue. They must practise the pronunciation of high heads, with or without a gradual fall, in which the unaccented syllables are adjusted to the immediately preceding accented syllable. For this purpose examples like the following may be used:

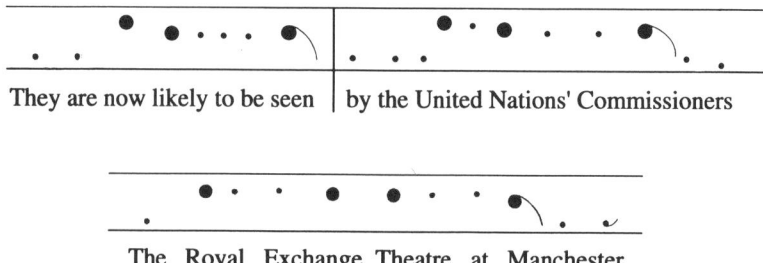

Transferring the weaving pattern to English at the end of tone groups has also unfortunate consequences. The intonation of the following example is neutral to Danish students but is strikingly marked to English listeners:

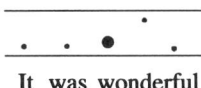

It was wonderful

In Danish the *pitch range* is normally rather narrow, and as British English characteristically employs a wide frequency spectrum, we can identify a second major difference between the intonational systems of the two languages. The difference lies essentially in English using, much more than Danish, the *high-pitch area*, i.e. the upper limit of the speaker's normal range of voice is considerably higher than in Danish. This can be observed most often in women, but it is also found in male speakers, some of whom may reach falsetto. The wide English pitch range is manifested in particular by the nucleus + tail (if any) moving over a considerable frequency area, and by the upward jump to the first syllable of the head being very strong. It is consequently important for Danes to practise a marked jump at the transition between the springboard and the head of the tone group. For this purpose examples of the following type may be used, in which the important transition between the first two components of the tone group is indicated by an arrow:

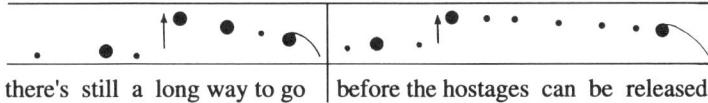

| there's still a long way to go | before the hostages can be released |

In tone groups which are spoken with falling or falling-rising contours and whose head is missing or falling, there is often a strong upward jump at the transition to the nucleus. The student must further realize that the head of a tone group with no springboard starts at a pitch that is very high to Danish ears:

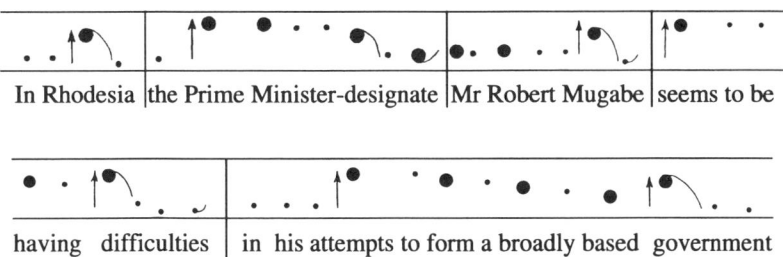

| In Rhodesia | the Prime Minister-designate | Mr Robert Mugabe | seems to be |

| having difficulties | in his attempts to form a broadly based government |

At the end of § 7.8 it was mentioned that narrowing of pitch range has a weakening effect in English and conveys attitudes like dejection, indifference or boredom. It follows that Danes should avoid transferring their habitual pitch ranges to English.

In Danish it is comparatively rare to find accented syllables pronounced with tone movement, with the result that the *nuclear glides* of English present a third major difficulty for Danes in the area of intonation. When Danish has something similar to English nuclei, i.e. a marked tone glide in an accented syllable, it is always in connection with emphasis. In practising strong tone glides in the nucleus of English tone groups, examples like the following may be used:

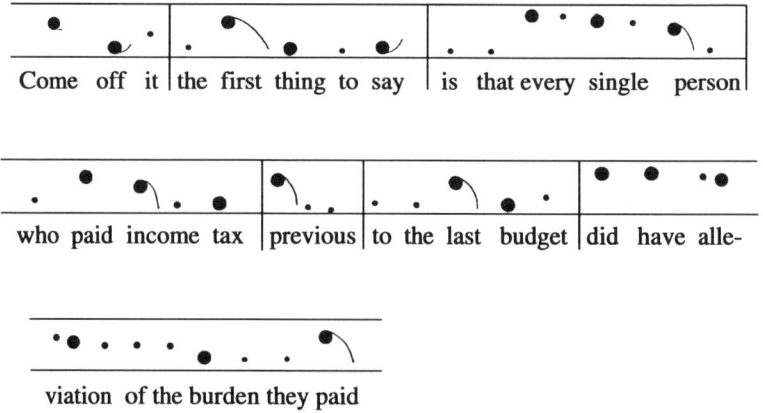

Of the English tone groups, the *falling-rising* type is unknown in Danish and nearly always causes difficulties. It is important to learn to identify and reproduce this tone-group type. To begin with, it is expedient to work with examples where the complex tone movement is distributed over a number of syllables:

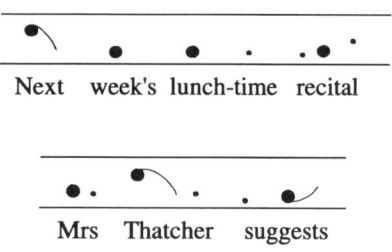

When Danish students have mastered the falling-rising pattern in utterances like these, they must try to pronounce the same pattern in its condensed form:

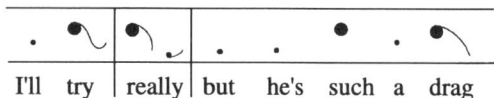

Finally it must be mentioned that *rising tone groups*, which are frequent in English, are uncommon in Danish. In Danish questions and incomplete parts of utterances, the accented syllables make up a tonal contour that is slightly falling, i.e. which only differs from the contour characteristic of final declarative utterances in falling to a lesser *degree*. Even in so-called statement questions, where the tonal contour is alone in signalling the status as question, a line drawn through the accented syllables is normally not rising but horizontal (cf. Thorsen 1978):

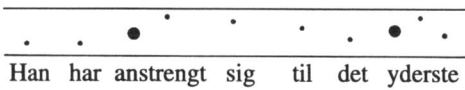

It follows that Danes must pay attention to the existence in English of tone groups that end in an upward movement:

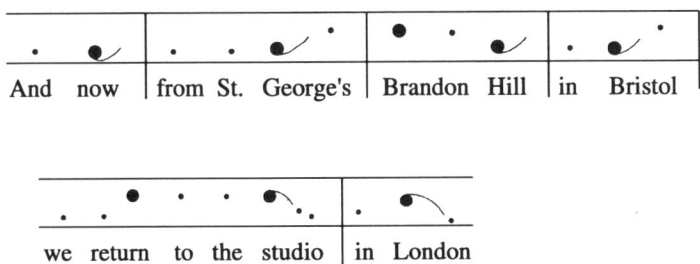

In conclusion, the special difficulties that English intonation presents to Danes can be repeated in the form of the following instructions, numbered according to importance:
(1) Avoid transferring the weaving Danish tonal pattern to English, and pronounce heads with the unaccented syllables on the same pitch level as the preceding accented syllable.
(2) Use a considerably wider pitch range than in Danish and make frequent use of the high-pitch area.
(3) Pronounce strong glides in the nuclei of tone groups.
(4) Learn to recognize and pronounce falling-rising tone groups.
(5) Learn to recognize and pronounce rising tone groups.

7.10. Simplified transcription

This section introduces a transcription system that uses so-called tonetic stress marks and which is easier to work with than the interlinear system. Let us first take a closer look at the four-level analysis of sentence accent suggested in § 7.5.

Primary accent is found only in the *nuclei* of tone groups. It must be emphasized that the dependency relation between primary accent and dynamic tonal prominence (always present in nuclei) is not a mutual one, for in one instance tone movement is not accompanied by the highest degree of accent: the up-glide often found on a syllable in the tail of a falling-rising tone group results in some tonal prominence, but as the stress is moderate and as the movement is restricted and dominated by the preceding strong down-glide, what we have here is one of the lower degrees of accent.

Secondary accent is found in the *first syllable of the head of a tone group* and in a *non-initial syllable of the head pronounced with an upward tone jump* (cf. § 7.7). In this connection it should be noted that other and less marked changes in pitch, e.g. the light downward jump on accented syllables in stepping falling heads, does not produce a secondary accent.

Tertiary accent is found in the *remaining accented syllables* of the tone group. As pointed out earlier, this degree of accent is connected with stress and distinct vowel quality and/or vowel length.

No accent is found in the remaining syllables of the tone group. As mentioned, unaccented syllables are pronounced without stress, and they are most often, though not always, characterized by blurred or lacking vowel quality.

These accentuations can be illustrated with the following example:

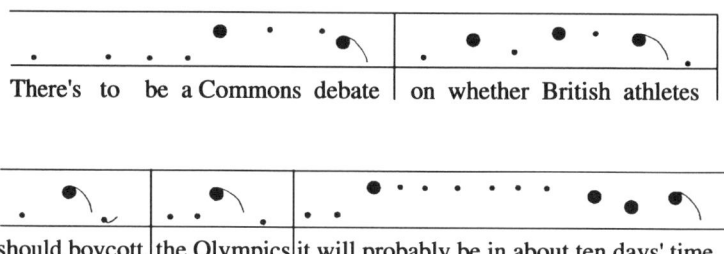

Primary accent occurs in the nuclei *(de)bate*, *ath(letes)*, *boy(cott)*, *(O)lym(pics)*, and *time*; secondary accent in *Com(mons)*, *wheth(er)*, *Brit(ish)*, and *prob(ably)*; tertiary accent in *ten* and *days'*; and no accent in the remaining syllables. Many of those remaining syllables are pronounced with blurred vowel quality, but there is a distinct vowel quality in *on*, *(ath)letes*, *(boy)cott*, and *(a)bout*, being pronounced with /ɒ/, /iː/, /ɒ/ and /aʊ/, respectively. It follows from the description here and in § 7.7 that there is this connection between the components of the tone group and accent: (1) In the springboard syllables are pronounced with no accent or tertiary accent. (2) In the head they are pronounced with secondary, tertiary or no accent. (3) The nucleus is pronounced with primary accent. (4) In the tail syllables are pronounced with no accent or tertiary accent.

We are now able to introduce the following simplified transcription system, which holds information about both intonation and accent:

(1) Primary accent as found in nuclei is symbolized with a preceding [\] (falling tone groups), [/] (rising tone groups), or [ˇ] (falling-rising tone groups).
(2) Secondary accent is symbolized with [ı].
(3) Tertiary accent is symbolized with [˙].
(4) No accent is indicated by the absence of a symbol.

In this simplified transcription system the example above can be notated as follows:

There's to be a ıCommons de\bate | on ıwhether ıBritish \athletes | should ˇboycott | the O\lympics | it will ı probably be in about ˙ten ˙days' \time

7.11. The use of the tone-group types

In § 7.8, on the basis of three contrasting pairs – certainty/uncertainty as to yes/no, kindness/unkindness, and completeness/incompleteness – we gave a characterization of the meaning and use of the tone-group types. That characterization was of a very general nature, and a more precise description presupposes a division of utterances into various categories. We shall now account for the use of the tone-group types taking five sentence categories as our point of departure. These categories have been established on a grammatical foundation, but the difference between them in grammatical form is generally accompanied by a difference in communicative function, which we shall also list:

(1) *Declarative sentences*
Grammatical characteristics: normal word order; presence of subject and of verb in finite form.
Main function: to inform about a fact, situation, circumstance, etc.
Example: *Peter is quite satisfied.*

(2) *Yes-no questions*
Grammatical characteristics: inversion or presence of a form of the auxiliary *do* before the subject.
Main function: to express lack of knowledge about a yes-no matter and request the listener to provide that knowledge.
Examples: *Is Peter quite satisfied?*
Do you really think that you'll do fine?

3) *Wh-questions*
Grammatical characteristics: introduced by an interrogative pronoun (including *how*); unless this realizes (part of) the subject, there is inversion or a form of the auxiliary *do* before the subject.
Main function: to express lack of knowledge about a specific matter in relation to place (*where*), time (*when*), cause (*why*), manner (*how*) or identity (*who, whom, which, what*) and request the listener to provide that knowledge.
Examples: *Who is quite satisfied?*
Where are you going?
How did she do it?

(4) *Imperatives*
Grammatical characteristics: presence of a verb in its base form; normally absence of surface subject.
Main function: to instruct the listener to behave in a certain manner, to perform a certain act, etc.
Example: *Make up your mind.*

(5) *Exclamations*
Grammatical characteristics: introduced by *what* or *how*; normal word order.
Main function: to signal a sudden emotional response.
Examples: *How delightful it looks!*
What a load of rubbish you're saying!

We shall include in this category exclamations without clause structure, consisting of a single word or a word group.
Examples: *Splendid!*
Good gracious!

While the capacity of the tone-group types to express completeness/incompleteness will not be discussed until the next section (about connected speech), both kindness/unkindness and certainty/uncertainty will be covered in the presentation here of some rules of intonation that can be posited for the five sentence categories. A few additional attitudinal dimensions will be included. For each sentence category the account below will proceed as follows: first it is stated which of the three tone-group types is/are normally used, i.e. is/are unmarked; then the use of other types is mentioned and the special effects connected with their use. To some extent pitch ranges will also be included.

Declarative sentences

Norm: falling intonation.
I did ˈall those ˈthings with a ˈcertain agˋgression
The ˈtrouble with ˈpolitics is that you're ˈshunted into ˋboxes
It's the ˈpeople who ˈwork in ˋsteel | who ˈreally ˋdo deˈpend on ˈmoney

Special effects: the *falling-rising* tone-group type is used especially to express a reservation (cf. § 7.8):

Well I ˈdidn't iˇnitially ˈrealize ˈthat

Falling intonation with *wide pitch range* is mainly used in emphatic utterances. In the following example the speaker emphasizes both nuclei by pronouncing them with a strong down-glide:

ˈYou are ˈactually ˈworse ˈoff than you were beˋfore | so we ˈhaven't ˈactually ˋgot inˈcreased inˈcentives

Rising intonation is used, for example, to express attitudes like uncertainty or kindness:

It ˈisn't eˈxactly what I ⁄want

The rising contour is also used when the function of a declarative sentence is not to inform but to ask the listener to state whether a matter is positive or negative. When declarative sentences are spoken with this intonation, they are called *statement questions*:

He ˈdoesn't re ´spect me?

In this connection *elliptical questions* ought to be mentioned because like statement questions they are spoken with rising intonation. An elliptical question functions as a request for information about positive-negative but the part that marks it syntactically as a yes-no question is left out:

ˈSame ´time?
In A ´merica?

As we have seen, a rising contour may signal uncertainty/kindness or a yes-no question. Consequently a declarative sentence pronounced with rising intonation is ambiguous and may give rise to misunderstanding ("Are you telling me or asking me?"). As a rule, however, the linguistic or situational context will enable the listener to decide whether one or the other function is intended.

Yes-no questions

Norm: rising or *falling-rising* intonation.
ˈWas it ˙disil´lusioning
ˈDidn't you ˋrealize | that ˈthey were ˙just as ˙nervous and un˙confident as ˇyou were
´Now | ˈisn't that ˋreally | your ˇtrouble ˙here

Special effects: falling intonation may convey a somewhat unkind attitude:

So ˈcould you ˙mention it to ˋhim | cos ˈI've in˙vited ˙him as ˋwell

Functionally the example (quoted from Crystal & Davy 1969) is close to a command. On the whole the falling tone-group type reduces the element of uncertainty as to positive-negative in yes-no questions. This can be seen also in the so-called *exclamatory questions*, which fall under the grammatical definition of yes-no questions, but whose primary function is to signal an emotional outburst:

ˈWasn't she ˋlovely!
ˈIsn't he ˋEnglish! (typically so)

Rising intonation with *wide pitch range* is used in *echo questions* (questions to the second power) which express amazement at the question asked:

(A: ˈAre you ´ready)   B: ˈAm I ´ready?!

A special type of yes-no question is constituted by the so-called *tag questions*. They combine a declarative construction, an imperative or an exclamation with a final appendage of the type *isn't it, has he* containing an auxiliary verb (including *be*) and a personal pronoun or *there*. Tag questions are spoken either as a *single tone group* of the falling-rising type or as *two tone groups* the second of which is pronounced with the falling pattern. The first of these possible pronunciations is used under the following conditions:

(1) Regularly if the tag follows an imperative:

ˈShut the ˇdoor ˙will you

(2) In the rather few cases where both the tag and a preceding construction are either positive or negative:

You'd ˇlike it ˙would you
He ˈcan't ˇcome ˙can't he

(3) If the speaker – although she considers it most likely that the addressee will agree with her – leaves it to the other person's discretion to answer yes or no to the question expressed by the tag and a preceding declarative construction:

There ˈwon't be ˇmany ˙will there

Tag questions are pronounced in the second way mentioned above under the following conditions:

(1) If the tag follows an exclamation:

How ˋwell she ˙sings | ˋdoesn't she

(2) If it is not left entirely to the addressee's discretion to answer yes or no but she is primarily asked to declare herself in agreement with the evaluation expressed in the declarative part of the construction:

ˈThis is the ˋtendency | ˋisn't it
You ˈdidn't ˙feel ˙very ˇwell | ˋ did you

In § 7.8 it was said that certainty/uncertainty as to yes or no plays an important part in the choice between the three tone-group types. As regards this contrasting pair, tag questions whose first part is a declarative construction fall between declarative sentences (falling intonation) and ordinary yes-no questions (rising or falling-rising intonation). If spoken with falling-rising intonation, they approach in content the latter of these sentence types; and if broken down into two tone groups the second of which is spoken with falling intonation, they approach the former. This relation can be illustrated with the following examples which constitute a scale of certainty/uncertainty:

ǀ This is the ˎtendency	Certain
ǀ This is the ˎtendency ǀ ˋisn't it	↑
ǀ This is the ˙tendency ˙isn't it	↓
Is ǀthis the ́tendency	Uncertain

Wh-questions

Norm: falling intonation.
ǀ What's the ˙worst ˙thing that could ˎhappen to you in ˙that ˙minefield
Now ǀ you ˙started ˎout ǀ with ǀvery ˙strong poˑlitical ˎviews ǀ ǀ how have ˎthey ˙changed
To ǀwhat exˎtent ǀ is your ǀattitude ˎto it ǀǀcoloured by the ˙fact that you ǀ have ˙broken a ˎway from it

Special effects: falling intonation with *wide pitch range* has an intensifying effect, and is used in emphatic wh-questions:

What on ǀearth are you ˎdoing

The *rising* tone-group type is used to express kindness, polite interest, etc:

ǀ What ˙time will you arˊrive

Finally, *rising* intonation with *wide pitch range* is used in wh-questions (including echo-questions) which have a manifest element of amazement:

ˊ What did you ˙say his ˙name was?!

Before we proceed to imperatives, we should mention that the rising tone-group type pronounced with wide pitch range almost invariably expresses astonished incredulity, an attitude that can be symbolized orthographically by question mark + exclamation mark. This is true not only of yes-no questions and wh-questions thus pronounced but also of many statement questions.

Imperatives

Norm: falling intonation.
ǀ Do as I ˎtell you
ǀ Try and ˙find aˎnother
ǀ I'm ˙very ˙much in ˙favour of inˎcentives ǀ but ǀlet's have in ˙centives for ˎeveryone

Special effects: the *rising* tone-group type – which is very common with this sentence category – is used when the speaker wants to make a request rather than issue a command. In other words, there is an element of appeal in imperatives when thus pronounced which results in a kinder impression:

ˈShut the ˊdoor ˙please
ˈJust ˙leave it to ˊme

Imperatives also occur with *falling-rising* intonation. This often signals an imploring attitude:

ˇDo be ˙careful
ˈWatch where you're ˇgoing

Exclamations

Norm: falling intonation.
ˋSplendid
ˈThanks ˙very ˋmuch
How inˈtensely anˋnoying
But ˈmy ˋgoodness | ˈthat's what ˙V.A.˙T. ˋdid

Special effects: this category is rarely spoken with anything but falling intonation, but one does find the *rising* tone-group type in some exclamations. This often expresses an encouraging attitude:

ˈWell ˊplayed
ˈGood ˊluck

This category also comprises *greetings* (*good night*, *hello*, etc.). While both *falling* and *rising* intonation are common in greetings exchanged when meeting, the latter is almost universal in goodbyes. The likely explanation is that the kindness indicated by the rising contour is a conventionally fitting element when concluding a conversation.

To exemplify greetings and elliptical questions we shall end by quoting the opening of an authentic telephone conversation (after Crystal & Davy 1969):

A: ˈHighview ˙double ˙three ˙four ˊfive   B: ˙Good ˋmorning
A: Helˋlo | ˊArthur   B: ˇValerie
A: ˋYes | ˙good ˋmorning   B: ˈThi…˙this is ˋArthur˙speaking
A: Helˋlo

It is of course possible to give a more thorough and detailed account of the use and meaning of the tone-group types in different sentence categories than provided here, and a book like O'Connor & Arnold (1973) operates with a much larger number of attitudes. In a brief introduction like ours, it seems a reasonable choice to limit the presentation to a broad outline. To conclude this section we present a table of the use of the tone-group types in which a plus indicates which type is the norm for a sentence category, and where particularly common alternative pronunciations are indicated by a plus in parentheses. The less characteristic uses, however, are ignored in the table; nor have pitch ranges been included:

	Declarative sentences	Yes-no questions	Wh- questions	Impera- tives	Exclama- tions
Falling:	+		+	+	+
Rising:		+	(+)	(+)	
Falling-rising:	(+)	+			

7.12. Connected tone groups

In the last section we dealt with the choice of tone-group type and pitch range in five sentence categories. On the whole we stayed within the boundaries of the single tone group. As imperatives and exclamations are nearly always short enough to be spoken as single tone groups, we shall have no more to say about those two categories. Some questions, however, and a very large number of declarative sentences are so long that they must be broken down into several tone groups. In these long sentences the last tone group is intoned in accordance with the rules formulated above, i.e. normally with rising or falling-rising intonation in yes-no questions and with falling intonation in declarative sentences and wh-questions. But what principles can be laid down for the tone groups preceding the last one? We shall now turn to that question and explain, for instance, the choices made in the non-final tone groups of examples like these:

I ˈdo deˇplore | this ˇtalk | of ˈgiving ˙money ˎback | to ˎwealthy ˙people
ˈDoes it ˎstill... | has ˎthat diˑminished | the ˇconsciousness of ˑclass
To ˈwhat exˎtent | is your ˈattitude ˎto it | ˈcoloured by the ˑfact that you ˈhave ˑbroken aˎway from it

As mentioned in § 7.8, there is some tendency in English to have rising or falling-rising intonation to indicate the incompleteness of *non-final* tone groups (*continuing intonation*) and to have falling intonation to indicate the completeness of *final* tone groups (*finishing intonation*). In the following examples the non-final tone groups (with a single exception) can be seen to be pronounced with continuing intonation:

ˇThis was proˑmoted | by the ˈEuropean ˑbroadcasting ˇunion | and ˇorganized | on the ˑunion's beˊhalf | by ˎFinnish ˑradio
And ˈthat ˑbrings to an ˊend | this ˊprogramme | by ˈAndrew ˑWatkinson vioˊlin | and ˈGordon ˎBack | piˎano

One of the constructions that clearly illustrate how intonation may express incompleteness is *enumeration*. Most commonly its first elements will be spoken with rising intonation (continuing intonation) and its last element with a fall (finishing intonation):

We went to ╱Cardiff | ╱Swansea | and ╲Wrexham

This is not the only possible pronunciation, however, and one often finds all elements in an enumeration spoken as rising tone groups. This signals that the enumeration as a whole is incomplete and could be continued. In the following long example, the upglide on the last element – *fringe benefits* – implies that further examples could be provided of the incentives of the rich to work:

And ׀let me ˙say ˙this about the ╲rich | that ׀they ˙don't ˙have to de╲pend on ˙money in ˙centives | because ׀they have ˙plenty of ╲other in ˙centives | they have the ad ׀vantage of ╱status | of ╱power | of ׀much ˙better ˙working con╱ditions | of pro׀motion ╱prospects | of ˙much ˙better ˙fringe ╱benefits | ׀they're the ╲last ˙ones | that ╲I ˙think | ׀need to have ˙extra ˙monetary in ╱centives | and ...

Alternative questions are intoned according to the same principles as enumerations. Most commonly the first half of the question is spoken with rising and the second half with falling intonation. This implies that a genuine alternative exists, i.e. the listener is requested to decide between the two choices offered:

׀Would you ˙like ╱claret | or ╲Burgundy

If the second half of the question is spoken as a rising or falling-rising tone group, i.e. with continuing intonation, the implication is that the addressee has more choices than those mentioned and may herself suggest something:

׀Would you ˙like ╱whisky | or ╱brandy (or something else?)

Or-questions consisting of more than two elements are also intoned along the same lines as enumerations (e.g. ╱coffee | ╱tea | or ╲cocoa).

Let us now inquire whether other principles than the contrasting pair completeness/incompleteness can be laid down for the distribution of the three intonation contours in connected speech. According to Crystal (1969:244ff) some tone groups are *subordinate* to other (preceding or following) tone groups. Subordinate tone groups are quite short and generally without head, have a narrower pitch range and less stress in the nucleus than the corresponding superordinate ones, and they are always spoken with the *same intonation pattern* as their superordinate partners. The phenomenon can be illustrated with the following examples, where the subordinate tone groups are in square brackets:

Now | you ˙started ↘out [you have ↘said] | with ...
the ↗views [of the ˙senti↗mentalists]
an [↘organized] ↘riot [at a ↘meeting]

The link between two tone groups of which one is subordinate to the other is closer than the link between two co-ordinate tone groups, and as a result of this close contact the boundary between them is hardly ever signalled by a pause (cf. § 7.7). As the following examples show (quoted from Crystal 1969:248), the difference between subordination and co-ordination is semantically relevant:

how ↘ever [˙this may ↘be]
how ↘ever | ˙this may ↘be

While the first tone-group sequence means 'however the case may be', the last means 'on the other hand – this may be true'.

The student of English must be prepared to subordinate some of her tone groups to others by pronouncing them with the same intonational pattern but with a narrower pitch range and less stress in the nucleus. For tone groups to lend themselves to this pronunciation they must consist of short sequences that are subordinate in content (e.g. less essential afterthoughts). Grammatically they are often appositional (cf. § 7.13), but as shown by the examples above, the pattern is also found with other syntactic structures.

Finally we must mention that the first tone group in a speaker's contribution is placed on a relatively *high pitch level* and spoken with a wider pitch range when a *new topic* is taken up. This is very common, for instance, in news reading:

there's ˙still a |long ˙way to ↘go | be˙fore the |hostages can be re↘leased |
(High pitch) There's to be a |Commons de↘bate | on |whether |British ↘athletes | should ˘boycott | the O↘lympics

The distribution of tone-group types in connected speech is a problematic area, and the principles laid down above must be regarded as *tendencies* rather than rules. In some cases a solution may be to break down long declarative sentences and wh-questions into the sequences ˘ + ˘ + ˘ + ... + ↘. In other cases a judicious mixture of the three tone-group types will be preferable in the non-final parts of long utterances. In making a decision, contrasting pairs like complete/incomplete and subordinate/co-ordinate may be helpful. But style and personal habits also come into play. Even if there is no system of fixed rules for the intonation of discourse, it remains necessary for the student to practise intonation in connected speech to accomplish the leap from an acceptable pronunciation of isolated groups to an equally acceptable pronunciation of tone-group sequences. In this connection it is important to pay attention to fluency, i.e. to ensure continuity between tone groups (which are not usually separated by regular pauses, cf. § 7.7).

7.13. Intonation and syntax

In the last two sections the point of departure for the description of the use of the tone-group types was largely grammatical, cf. how sentence categories were established and how grammatical constructions like alternative questions and enumerations were put to use. Even though the intonation of English is determined by factors other than grammatical ones, there is a close connection between intonation and syntax. This connection will be further illustrated in the present section where we will focus on the intonation patterns of some selected grammatical constructions.

Apposition

By apposition is meant the addition of a word or word group to a preceding word or word group as an explanatory extension. The most typical examples of apposition consist of two nouns or noun groups with identical reference. In pronunciation these are treated as two tone groups of the same type, i.e. there is *tonal concord*:

ˑMr ˎSchultz | our ˌnew ˎmanager | is a ˎGerman
ˌDid you ˑsee ˑMr ˊSchultz | our ˌnew ˊmanager
ˑMr ˇSchultz | our ˌnew ˇmanager | preˌfers ˎWagner
I ˌdon't ˎthink you ˑsee | that ˌany proˎgressive ˑgovernment | a ˎLabour ˑgovernment | could ˌpossibly have ˎdone it

Besides having the same intonation contour as the preceding tone group, an appositional element is often spoken as a *subordinate* tone group (cf. the last section). In all the sentences above this would be a natural solution if the speaker considers the appositional extension to be subordinate in content. Tonal concord + subordination can be illustrated with the following examples:

ˇNext ˑweek's ˑlunchtime reˑcital | ... is ˌgiven by ˑBenjamin ˊLuxon [ˇbaritone] | and ˌDavid ˎWillison [piˎano]
Do you ˇfeel that ˑstrongly [ˇconsciously]

Relative clauses

A *non-restrictive* (or *parenthetical*) relative clause is in apposition to the noun or noun group in the superordinate clause that it modifies. In the light of what we have just seen, it is not surprising that constructions of this type also normally have *tonal concord*, i.e. the same tone-group type as that of the antecedent:

ˑMr ˇSchultz | who ˑcomes from Baˇvaria | is a draˌmatic ˎtenor
ˌThen they ˑserved us ˎguinea-ˑfowl | which I disˎlike

Non-restrictive relative clauses are *always* separated from their antecedent by a tone-group boundary. In this they differ from restrictive relative clauses, which are most often spoken without a preceding tone-group boundary:

ꞌWhat's the ˙worst ˙thing that could ˎhappen to you in ˙that ˙minefield

When a restrictive relative clause is separated from the antecedent by a tone-group boundary, this is usually because antecedent and relative clause together make up a word group of such *length* that they are hard to pronounce as one tone group:

I've ꞌjust had aˑglimpse of the ˇnewly-ˑweds | you deꞌscribed to me ˑyesterday ˎmorning ˑCecily

Occasionally, however, one encounters restrictive relative clauses that are detached from their antecedent in rather short constructions, i.e. where a pronunciation without a tone-group boundary would not result in excessively long tone groups. This can be observed in the following examples, where it may further be noticed that one of the relative clauses has been broken down into two groups:

And you ꞌsimply ˇcan't ˑtackle inˑflation | if you ˎspend ˑmoney | which you ˑhaven't ˎgot
ꞌThey're the ˎlast ˑones | that ˎI ˑthink | ꞌneed to have ˑextra ˑmonetary inˊcentives

In non-restrictive relative clauses not only a preceding but also a *following* tone-group boundary is obligatory, i.e. these clauses are always treated as *independent tone groups* (or as sequences of independent tone groups). A following boundary, however, is not obligatory with restrictive relative clauses, which are frequently integrated into the same tone group as both the antecedent and a following predicate. Presence/absence of tone-group boundaries around relative clauses may be illustrated with the following example:

The ꞌsoldiers who were ˑbrave ˑran ˎforward
The ˇsoldiers | who were ˇbrave | ˑran ˎforward

In the first of these the intonation unequivocally marks the relative clause as restrictive, i.e. the meaning is '(only) those soldiers who were brave ran forward'. In contrast, there is every likelihood that the intonation contour of the last example will make the listener interpret it as non-restrictive, i.e. perceive the meaning to be '(all) the soldiers – and brave they were – ran forward'.

Sentence adverbials

By 'adverbial' is meant a syntactic constituent with adverbial function consisting of one or more words, and by 'sentence adverbial' is meant an adverbial that modifies a sentence as a whole. Unlike other adverbials, which are integrated into a sentence by being a modification of an element of it, e.g. a verb or an adjective, sentence adverbials are *loosely attached* to the sentence they appear in, i.e. their status is *peripheral.* Examples of sentence adverbials are *actually, apparently, clearly, frankly, honestly, however, really* and *as it were, of course, so to speak, to be sure*. When a sentence adverbial is *initial* in a sentence, it is normally spoken as an independent tone group of the falling-rising type:

ˇActually | there's ⁱnot a ˙hell of a ˙lot ˋto it

In *final* position this is not the case. Here sentence adverbials are usually intoned as the tail – or as part of the tail – of the preceding tone group:

Iˡ wasn't ˋworrying for ˙Christ's ˙sake
ˡGot to ˇoffer her ˙some ˙actually

Sentence adverbials consisting of several words, as well as certain single-word sentence adverbials (*though, however*) are also placed in the tail of a tone group when they occur in *medial* position:

They ˋhave of ˙course | ˙pulled ˙off a ˙diploˇmatic ˙victory
You'll ˡprobably aˇgree ˙though | that it's a ˡmonstrous proˋposal

The rules posited here for the pronunciation of sentence adverbials in the three positions are not without exceptions. That is apparent in the following where the speaker underlines *obviously* by pronouncing it as an independent tone group:

Well I ˡdidn't iˇnitially ˙realize ˙that | ˇobviously | but ...

We must also mention the fact that some adverbials may function as both sentence adverbials and adverbials of manner. This difference in syntactic function (peripheral versus integrated status) is normally conveyed by a difference in intonation to the effect that a finally placed adverbial of manner is pronounced in the nucleus of the tone group, a sentence adverbial in the tail. The distinction can be illustrated with the following example:

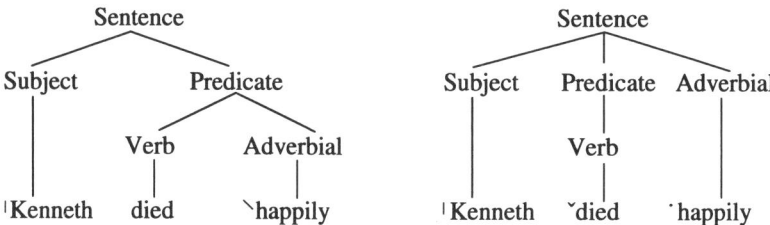

In the diagram to the left, where the adverbial modifies *died* and is placed in the nucleus (+ tail) of the tone group, *happily* is an adverbial of manner meaning 'in a happy manner'. In the diagram to the right, where there is sentence modification and position in the tail, it is a sentence adverbial meaning 'fortunately'.

136

Vocatives, reporting clauses, and comment clauses

By *vocative* we understand a word or a word group used as a term of address, i.e. proper nouns or common nouns used as names, whether with or without modification, such as *Joyce, Mr Crocker-Harris, sweet Simon, sir, darling, my love, you stupid idiot*. Intonationally vocatives behave like sentence adverbials. In initial position they usually constitute an independent tone group (often of the falling-rising type), but medially and finally – where they occur more frequently – they are added to the preceding tone group as (part of) its tail. We can illustrate this with the following examples:

ˇBrenda | I ˈthink I could ˙do with a ˙glass of ˎsherry
ˈCan't you ˎsee you ˙idiot | it's ˙what she ˎwants
ˎRubbish ˙man | ˈnothing ˎto it
I should ˇthink so ˙darling
ˈDo ˙please ˙shut ˎup ˙Morris
ˈYou ˙go ˙on as ˙long as you ˇlike my ˙dear
I'm ˈnot ˙letting you ˙run ˊon ˙old ˙boy
ˈYou ˙did ˎwell ˙Terence | ˈyou ˎtoo ˙Mrs ˙Chudleigh

Reporting clauses are phrases like *she then says, he added*, etc., whose function is to signal direct speech. These are also intoned in the same way as sentence adverbials:

ˈThen she ˙says as to an ˇimbecile | your liˎbido | your ˈsexual ˎdrive
How ˇlong he ˙then ˙asks | have you been ˙letting them ˙in at ˎyour ˙place
ˈFirst ˇme | ˈthen ˎyou re˙plied ˙Kelly

As appears from the examples above, the tone groups in which medial/final vocatives or reporting clauses constitute the tail, may be falling, falling-rising, or rising. This is also true of tone groups whose tail contains sentence adverbials. The choice of tone-group type is not conditioned by these attached elements but is made according to the principles explained in § 7.11 and § 7.12.

By *comment clauses* we understand structures which consist of a personal pronoun (first or second person singular) and a verb (+ any other constituents), and which like sentence adverbials, vocatives and reporting clauses are loosely attached to the superordinate clauses that they modify. As examples may be mentioned *you see, you know, mind you, you must admit* and *I gather, I admit, I'm sure, I'm afraid, I dare say*. Many comment clauses are set expressions that are inserted in running speech to establish an informal contact with the listener. The *I*-clauses signal specific attitudes (of concession, obligation, (un)certainty, etc.), and the *you*-clauses are often an appeal to the listener to pay attention. In medial and final position, comment clauses are intoned like sentence adverbials, vocatives and reporting clauses, i.e. they are attached to the preceding tone group as (part of) its tail:

I ˋdo I'm aˑfraid | ˈrather ˑact on ˋimpulse
Eˈmotionally you ˇwere I iˑmagine | and ˈstill ˋare
ˈNot that there's a ˑlot of ˋdifference I aˑgree
To exˑpress e╱motion you ˑmean
It ˈwasn't ˑalways like ˋthat I ˑpromise you
It's ˋprivate you ˑsee
They'll ˈknow whether she's aˈlive or ˇdead I iˑmagine
We have ˈno ˑwhite ˑcoats ˋhere you'll have ˑnoticed

In initial position it is most common for a *you*-clause to form an independent tone group and for an *I*-clause to be integrated into the following clause by being pronounced as part of the same tone group:

ˇMind you | it ˈisn't ˑjust emˋbarrassment
I ˑthink this is ˈawfully ˋsad

8. SOUND COMBINATIONS

8.1. Assimilation

When the various vowels and consonants of English are pronounced in immediate succession in words and sentences, they are often changed considerably by the process of *assimilation*. A distinction is made between *progressive* and *regressive* assimilation according to the direction of the process: in progressive assimilation a sound is changed under the lingering influence of a preceding segment; in regressive assimilation a sound is changed in anticipation of a following segment. The two types of assimilation can be illustrated with the following examples:

[pn] → [pm] in *happen* (progressive)
[vt] → [ft] in *have to* (regressive)

In the first example the labiality of [p] is preserved during the pronunciation of the nasal, and in the last example the voicelessness of [t] is anticipated in the pronunciation of the fricative.

Assimilations may also be categorized as *phonemic* and *non-phonemic*. Both examples above are phonemic: in the sequence *have to*, where [v] is changed to [f], the phoneme boundary between /v/ and /f/ is crossed; similarly, if *happen* is pronounced ['hæpm], we have a different phoneme sequence than in ['hæpn]. In a sequence like *thank you*, on the other hand, [j] is devoiced to [j̊] because of the preceding voiceless plosive, and as both sounds manifest the phoneme /j/, we have a non-phonemic case. Non-phonemic assimilations that result in particularly clear conditioned variants, like devoiced [j̊], [l̥] and fronted [u:] in *thank you*, *please* and *music*, were treated in Chapters 5 and 6 under the individual phonemes and will not be discussed further.

Finally, assimilation may be categorized as *word-internal* and *word-external*. The former refers to assimilations taking place within the boundaries of a word independently of whatever phonetic surroundings the word may be appearing in. We had word-internal assimilation in *happen* above (when pronounced ['hæpm]); a parallel example is *bacon*, where besides ['beɪkən, 'beɪkn] there is an alternative pronunciation ['beɪkŋ] in which the alveolar [n] has been changed to the velar [ŋ] because of the preceding velar stop. Word-internal assimilation has been a common process in the history of the language; in a case like *husband* (/'hʌzbənd/) an original [s] has changed to [z] under the influence of the following voiced [b]. (All of these three cases of word-internal assimilation are phonemic: /n/ → /m/, /n/ → /ŋ/ and /s/ → /z/; non-phonemic examples above were *please* and *music*.) Word-external assimilation refers to a process in connected speech which works across word boundaries and only effects changes in word-marginal segments. Cases above were *have to* (regressive and phonemic) and *thank you* (progressive and non-phonemic). We can also illustrate with the word sequence *of course*, where the final [v] of the first word is devoiced to [f] by the initial [k] of the second word ([əf 'kɔːs], regressive and phonemic), and with the sequence *could you?*, where the initial palatal [j] is changed to the palato-alveolar fricative element [ʒ] under the influence of the final alveolar [d] of the first word (['kʊdʒʊ], progressive and phonemic).

Below we shall survey some of the most important phonemic, word-external assimilations in English.

(1) *Assimilations as to voice.* – Of the assimilations affecting the voicing of a sound, two are particularly important:

[v] → [f] before voiceless consonants
[z] → [s] after voiceless consonants

We can exemplify the first of these developments with *have to* and *of course*. The words *have* and *of* are pronounced in isolation with [v], but when followed by a word with an initial voiceless consonant, [v] may be devoiced to [f] by regressive assimilation (['hæftʊ, əf 'kɔːs]). The assimilation of [z] to [s] can be exemplified with *the cat's dead* and *it's been a long time*. The verb forms *is* and *has* are pronounced with [z] when isolated, but when contracted with a preceding word that ends in a voiceless sound, and after [h] and the vowels are lost, there is devoicing of [z] to [s] through progressive assimilation ([kæts, ɪts]). The progressive assimilation of *s*-endings is an obligatory process in English (cf. § 2.3).

(2) *Assimilations as to place of articulation.* – Word-final alveolar consonants are frequently assimilated to a following sound which is articulated further forward or back in the mouth. Among these developments the following are the most important:

[s] → [ʃ] before [j, ʃ]
[z] → [ʒ] before [j, ʃ]

The first can be exemplified with the word sequences *miss you* and *this ship*, where the alveolar [s] may be changed to the palato-alveolar [ʃ] under the influence of a palatal and a palato-alveolar consonant respectively (['mɪʃ jʊ, 'ðɪʃ 'ʃɪp]). The corresponding retraction of [z] can be illustrated with the examples *please you* and *was sure* (['pliːʒ jʊ, wəʒ 'ʃʊə]). In rapid speech [-ʒʃ-] may develop further to [-ʃʃ-] through voice assimilation, so that e.g. *was sure* and *is she?* may also be pronounced [wəʃ 'ʃʊə, 'ɪʃ ʃɪ].

The following progressive assimilations as to place of articulation are also common in English:

[t j] → [tʃ]
[d j] → [dʒ]

In both of these cases the palatal [j] is changed under the influence of a preceding alveolar to a palato-alveolar fricative element (the affricated release stage of a palato-alveolar stop), being moreover devoiced in the one case. Examples of these developments are *can't you?* and *could you?* which in rapid speech are pronounced ['kɑ:ntʃʊ, 'kʊdʒʊ].

Finally the phenomenon of *elision* should be mentioned. By this is understood an assimilatory loss of a sound segment. If e.g. [d] in the word sequence *send money* is to be assimilated to the surroundings, the only possibility is to exchange the orality of the sound with nasality, and in rapid speech that is equal to loss (['send 'mʌnɪ → 'senn 'mʌnɪ → 'sen 'mʌnɪ]). Elision may be characterized as 'assimilation to zero'.

Among the important *consonant elisions* in English is the loss of [t] and [d] between preceding and following consonants. Examples are *next best, just now, kept quiet* (['neks(t) 'best, 'dʒʌs(t) 'naʊ, 'kep(t) 'kwaɪət]) and *hold together, old boy, found fault* (['həʊl(d) tə'geðə, 'əʊl(d) 'bɔɪ, 'faʊn(d) 'fɔ:lt]). In compounds we find the same elision of alveolar plosives under these conditions, cf. examples like *coast-line, dustbin* and *sandbag, landslide* (['kəʊs(t)laɪn, 'dʌs(t)bɪn, 'sæn(d)bæg, 'læn(d)slaɪd]). Also common is the loss of [h] in form words like *he, him, her, have, has, had, who* when they are unaccented and not initial in a sentence (cf. the lists of weak forms in § 6.9). A sentence like *you should have helped him*, for instance, is normally pronounced [jʊ ʃʊd əv 'helpt ɪm].

The most common *vowel elision* is the loss of [ə] before [r] and [l]. As examples may be given *preferable, lavatory, carefully* and *chancellor*, pronounced by many speakers of English ['prefrəbl, 'lævətrɪ, 'keəflɪ, 'tʃɑ:nslə] instead of ['prefərəbl, 'lævətərɪ, 'keəfəlɪ, 'tʃɑ:nsələ]. In rapid speech this type of elision is also found in syllables to the left of the main accent, cf. examples like *gorilla* and *police* pronounced ['grɪlə, 'pli:s] instead of [gə'rɪlə, pə'li:s]. Elision of [ə] in connected speech is evidenced in particular before a 'linking r', as in *matter of fact* and *better and better* (['mæt(ə)r əv 'fækt, 'bet(ə)r ən 'betə]).

8.2. The English syllable

As mentioned in § 5.1, the syllable is a phonetic unit that is registered directly and spontaneously by the listener. When you listen to any English utterance, you observe a number of small peaks which differ from the surroundings by being especially sonorous, and it is those *peaks of sonority* that are decisive for the perception of syllables. In a word like /tə'bækənɪst/ (*tobacconist*) the vowels /ə, æ, ə, ɪ/ create four such syllabic peaks, while the remaining and less sonorous sound segments are perceived as valleys in between. The sonority of a sound depends primarily on its degree of opening, and consequently the peak of the syllable is normally formed by vowels, which are produced with a relatively open vocal tract, while consonants, being articulated with a more constricted vocal tract, form the valley.

In addition to the phonetic description above, the syllable may be characterized as the unit to which accent is attached, cf. examples like *billow/below* (and Danish *billigst/bilist*).

It is possible to base an account of the structure of the English syllable on existing *monosyllabic words* because their syllabic structures are representative, i.e. identical to those occurring in polysyllabic words and in connected speech. An investigation of monosyllabic words shows that the syllabic structure of English can be captured by the following formula:

$$C_{0-3} \, V \, C_{0-4}$$

The formula says that besides the obligatory vocalic element (V) there may be up to three initial consonants (C_{0-3}) and up to four final consonants (C_{0-4}). The following examples illustrate the options:

	Initially			Finally	
ape	/eɪp/	-VC	*fee*	/fi:/	CV-
rape	/reɪp/	CVC	*feel*	/fi:l/	CVC
crape	/kreɪp/	CCVC	*field*	/fi:ld/	CVCC
scrape	/skreɪp/	CCCVC	*fields*	/fi:ldz/	CVCCC
			texts	/teksts/	CVCCCC

The two extreme syllable structures $C_0 \, V \, C_0$ and $C_3 \, V \, C_4$ can be exemplified with *are* (/ɑ:/) and the plural form *strengths* which may be pronounced /streŋkθs/ besides the more common form /streŋθs/. Note that the first of three initial consonants in a syllable is always /s/, that the last of three final consonants is normally one of the inflectional suffixes /-z, -s, -d, -t/, and that the last of four final consonants is always one of the suffixes /-s, -t/.

The structure of English syllables normally follows the *sonority principle*, according to which the peak of the syllable is flanked by sound segments with gradually decreasing sonority; when several consonants occur to the left or right of the peak, the nearest will be relatively sonorous (sonorants) while those farther removed will have lower sonority (obstruents). The syllable is thus characterized by a rising and falling sonority curve, which can be illustrated with the following diagram where V stands for 'vowel', S for 'sonorant', and O for 'obstruent':

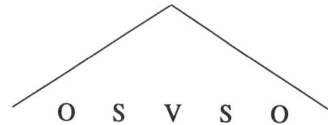

Examples of syllables with this structure are the words /prɪns, blʌnt, drɪŋk, ʃrɪmp, kweɪnt, smaɪlz/ (*prince, blunt, drink, shrimp, quaint, smiles*). The sonority principle is clearly reflected in the combinatory possibilities of the sonorants. Syllable-initially they can all (except /ŋ/ which does not occur in this position) be combined with preceding consonants. Syllable-finally those sonorants that occur (/m, n, ŋ, l/) may all be combined with following consonants, but apart from /m/ and /n/, which may follow /l/ as in *film, kiln*, they do not enter into combinations with preceding consonants.

ANNOTATED BIBLIOGRAPHY

Linguistics and general phonetics

Catford, J.C. (1988) *A Practical Introduction to Phonetics*. Oxford: Clarendon Press.
Explains how speech sounds are produced.

Clark, J. & Yallop, C. (1995) *An Introduction to Phonetics and Phonology*, 2nd edition. Oxford: Blackwell.
Comprehensive treatment of the articulation and acoustics of speech and of phonological analysis. For teachers rather than students.

Crystal, D. (1987) *The Cambridge Encyclopedia of Language*. Cambridge: University Press.
Highly useful survey of most aspects of languages and linguistics. Scholarly and popular at the same time; many illustrations.

Crystal, D. (1991) *A Dictionary of Linguistics and Phonetics*, 3rd edition. Oxford: Blackwell.

Ladefoged, P. (1993) *A Course in Phonetics*, 3rd edition. New York: Harcourt Brace.
Excellent general introduction.

O'Connor, J.D. (1973) *Phonetics*. Harmondsworth: Penguin.
Accessible presentation of phonetic concepts, with exemplification mostly from English.

Roach, P. (1992) *Introducing Phonetics*. Harmondsworth: Penguin.

The pronunciation of English

Bauer, L., Dienhart, J.M., Hartvigson, H.H. & Jakobsen, L.K. (1980) *American English Pronunciation*. Copenhagen: Gyldendal. With a separate *Supplement: Comparison with Danish*.
Textbook primarily aimed at Danish students of English. A special feature is a consistent comparison of American with British English pronunciation.

Crystal, D. (1995) *The Cambridge Encyclopedia of the English Language*. Cambridge: University Press.
This invaluable volume contains much on the sound system of English, its historical development and present-day variation.

Davidsen-Nielsen, N. (1970) *Engelsk fonetik*. Copenhagen: Gyldendal.

Textbook on the pronunciation of British English. Larger than the present book but does not cover intonation.

Gimson, A.C. (1994) *Gimson's Pronunciation of English*, 5th edition, revised by A. Cruttenden. London: Edward Arnold.
The standard work on British English. Describes so-called Received Pronunciation, but has much on variation. There is also a historical chapter.

Knowles, G.O. (1987) *Patterns of Spoken English: An Introduction to English Phonetics*. London: Longman.
Course book with exercises. Emphasis on rhythm and intonation.

Livbjerg, I. & Mees, I.M. (1997) *Practical English Phonetics: Ny kontrastiv fonetik*, 2nd edition. Copenhagen: Schønberg.
For Danish students who want to improve their pronunciation of English. Contrastive analyses, exercises; tape.

Mees, I.M. & Collins, B. (1996) *Sound English: A Practical Pronunciation Guide for Speakers of Danish*, 2nd edition. Copenhagen: Nyt Nordisk Forlag Arnold Busck.

Roach, P. (1991) *English Phonetics and Phonology: A Practical Course*, 2nd edition. Cambridge: University Press.
Good basic course book with exercises and tapes. There are suggestions for further reading throughout.

Prosody

Bradford, B. (1988) *Intonation in Context: Intonation practice for upper-intermediate and advanced learners of English.* Cambridge: University Press.
With accompanying tape.

Cruttenden, A. (1986) *Intonation.* Cambridge: University Press.
Theoretical textbook for students of linguistics.

Crystal, D. (1969) *Prosodic Systems and Intonation in English.* Cambridge: University Press.
A major work in the field. Not too easy to read.

Davidsen-Nielsen, N. (1984) *Tonegangen i Britisk Engelsk.* Copenhagen: Albion.
The sections on intonation in the present book are based on Davidsen-Nielsen (1984), and the accompanying tape includes the examples used in the present book.

Fudge, E.C. (1984) *English Word Stress.* London: Allen & Unwin.
Standard work on this aspect of the prosodic system.

O'Connor, J.D. & Arnold, G. (1973) *Intonation of Colloquial English: A Practical Handbook*, 2nd edition. London: Longman.
A standard work; with extensive exemplification and accompanying tapes.

Varieties of spoken English

Crystal, D. & Davy, D. (1969) *Investigating English Style*. London: Longman.

Honey, J. (1989) *Does Accent Matter: The Pygmalion Factor*. London: Faber and Faber.
On attitudes to Received Pronunciation and other accents. Easy reading but very informative.

Hughes, A. & Trudgill, P. (1996) *English Accents and Dialects: An Introduction to Social and Regional Varieties of British English*, 3rd edition. London: Edward Arnold.
A short and easy introduction. With accompanying tape.

Juul, A., Nielsen, H.F. & Sørensen, K., eds. (1988) *Degeneration on the Air?* Copenhagen: Landscentralen for Undervisningsmidler/Danmarks Lærerhøjskole.
Texts from the long-standing debate about the quality of English on BBC radio. With eight tapes.

Ramsaran, S., ed. (1990) *Studies in the Pronunciation of English: A commemorative volume in honour of A.C. Gimson*. London: Routledge.
A collection of specialist articles.

Trudgill, P. & Hannah, J. (1994) *International English: A Guide to Varieties of Standard English*, 3rd edition. London: Edward Arnold.
Brief descriptions ranging from Received Pronunciation and other British varieties to North American and non-native. Pronunciation well covered. With tape.

Wells, J.C. (1982) *Accents of English*, Vol. 1 *An Introduction*, Vol 2 *The British Isles*, Vol. 3 *Beyond the British Isles*. Cambridge: University Press.
A comparative survey of the many geographical and social varieties of English pronunciation. With accompanying tape.

The pronunciation of Danish

Becker-Christensen, C. (1987) *Bogstav og lyd. Dansk retskrivning og rigsmålsudtale*, vol. 1. Copenhagen: Gyldendal.

Brink, L. & Lund, J. (1974) *Udtaleforskelle i Danmark, aldersbestemte, geografiske, sociale*. Copenhagen: Gjellerup.

Entertaining account of generational, regional and social variation in the pronunciation of Danish.

Grønnum, N. (1992) *The Groundworks of Danish Intonation: An Introduction.* Copenhagen: Museum Tusculanum Press.
Summary of thesis, incorporating a number of specialist articles. A forerunner was Thorsen (1978).

Grønnum, N. (1998) *Fonetik og Fonologi. Almen og Dansk.* Copenhagen: Akademisk Forlag.
Textbook for first-year university students.

Hansen, E. & Lund, J. (1983) *Sæt tryk på. Syntaktisk tryk i dansk.* Lærerforeningernes Materialeudvalg.

Heger, S. (1981) *Sprog og lyd: Elementær dansk fonetik.* Copenhagen: Akademisk forlag.
A description of modern Danish standard pronunciation. With a chapter on social variation.

Thorsen, N. (1978) An acoustical investigation of Danish intonation. *Journal of Phonetics* 6, 151-175.
An experimental investigation of the intonation of modern East/Copenhagen Danish.

Learning and teaching pronunciation

Brazil, D., Coulthard, M. & Johns, C. (1980) *Discourse Intonation and Language Teaching.* London: Longman.
How intonation contributes to the communicative value of speech, and how the contours may be taught. With tape.

Brown, A., ed. (1991) *Teaching English Pronunciation: A Book of Readings.* London: Routledge.
A wide range of articles, many by renowned experts in the field of foreign language teaching.

Brown, G. (1990) *Listening to Spoken English*, 2nd edition. London: Longman.
How normal conversational English differs from the form usually described, and how listening comprehension may be taught.

Davidsen-Nielsen, N., Færch, C. & Harder, P. (1982) *The Danish Learner.* English Language Teachers' Manuals 1. Tunbridge Wells: Anthony Taylor.
The problems Danes encounter in speaking English. One third of the book is on pronunciation.

Færch, C., Haastrup, K. & Phillipson, R. (1984) *Learner Language and Language Learning*. Copenhagen: Gyldendal.
On the 'interlanguage' of Danish learners and their communication strategies. Includes a chapter on pronunciation.

Lee, W.R. (1964) Linguistics and phonetics in the training of teachers of English. In *In Honour of Daniel Jones*, ed. D. Abercrombie et al. London: Longman.

Livbjerg, I. & Mees, I. (1995) Segmental errors in the pronunciation of Danish speakers of English: some pedagogic strategies. In *Studies in General and English Phonetics*, ed. J.W. Lewis, 432-444. London: Routledge.
This article has many useful observations on pronunciation errors which have received too much attention, and on neglected areas and false descriptions.

Pike, K.L. (1967) *Phonetics*. Ann Arbor: The University of Michigan Press.

Dictionaries of pronunciation

Jones, D. (1997) *English Pronouncing Dictionary*, 15th edition, edited by P. Roach & J. Hartman. Cambridge: University Press.
A standard dictionary of British English pronunciation. This edition also covers American pronunciation.

Kenyon, J.S. & Knott, T.A. (1982) *A Pronouncing Dictionary of American English*, 4th edition. Springfield: Merriam; London: Longman.
The authoritative dictionary of American English pronunciation.

Pointon, G.E. (1983) *BBC Pronouncing Dictionary of British Names*, 2nd edition. Oxford: University Press.

Wells, J.C. (1990) *Longman Pronunciation Dictionary*. London: Longman.
Competes with Jones (1997). Covers both British and American pronunciation.

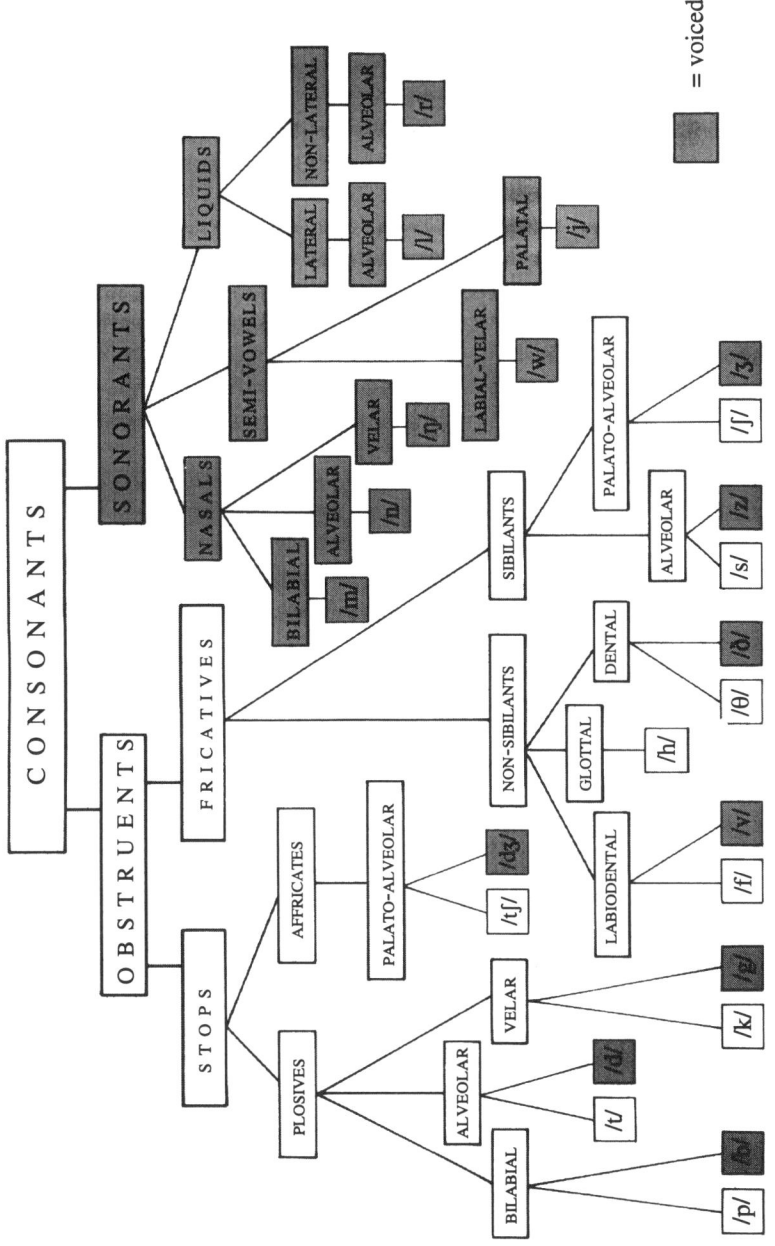

Table 1

English monophthongs

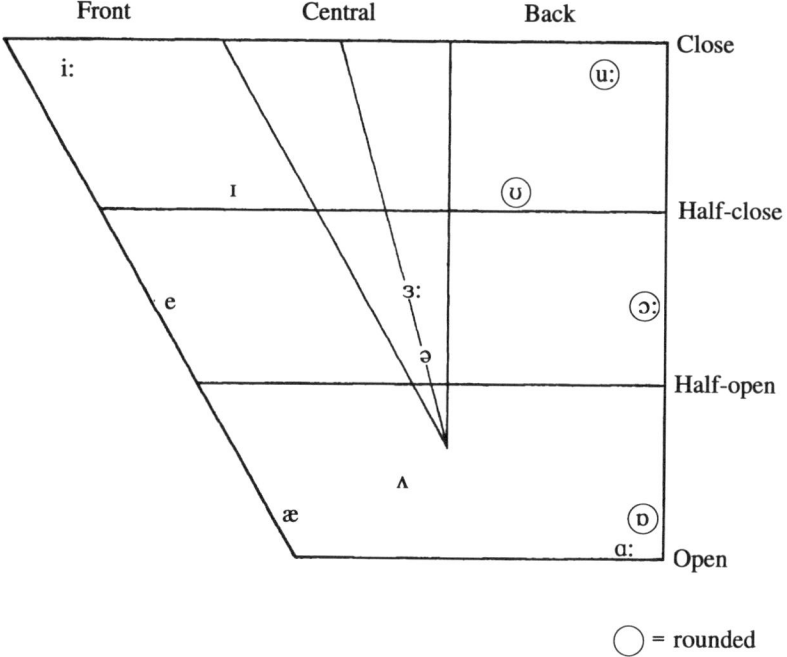

Table 2

INDEX

absolute pitch 111
accent 97f
   – in compounds 104f
   distinctive function of – 99
   main – 99f
   no – 99f, 107f, 124
   – in polysyllabic words 100f
   primary – 107f, 123f
   rhythmically conditioned – 102
   secondary – 107f, 123f
   sentence – 107f
   subsidiary – 99f, 102f
   tertiary – 107f, 124
   unitary – 104f
   word – 100f
accent-timed rhythm 109f
accentual
   – pattern 100
   – system 99f
acoustic phonetics 11
active articulator 14
advanced nucleus 115f
affricated stops, affricates 31f
affrication 35
allophone, allophonic variant 19
alphabetic, phonemic writing 27
alternative questions 132
alveolar 32f
alveolar ridge 13f
analytic approach 23
antepenult rule 101f
applied phonetics 23f
apposition 134
articulation
   manner of – 14
   place of – 14f
   speed of – 109
articulator 14
articulatory
   – phonetics 11
   – system 13f

aspiration 36f
assimilation 139f
   – as to place 140
   – as to voice 140
attitudinal function of intonation 112
auditory phonetics 11
auxiliary verbs
   vowel alternation 92f

back-closing diphthongs 66
back of tongue 13f
back vowels 63f, 66
bilabial 32f
blade of tongue 13f

cardinal vowels 64f
central vovels 63f, 66
centre of tongue 13f
centring diphthongs 66
certainty/uncertainty 116f, 125f
clear [l] 57f
close vowels 63, 66f
closing stage 35
comment clauses 137f
communication process 11
commutable 17f
commutation test 18
complementary distribution 19
completeness/incompleteness 116f, 125f
compounds 104f
   verb + adverb 105
   vowel alternation 91f
compression stage 35
conditioned allophone 19
connected tone groups 131f
consonant elision 141
consonants 29f, 149
   Danish – 33f
   inventory of – 30f
   system of – 31f
   voiced – 32f

voiceless – 32f
content, lexical words 94
continuing intonation 131f
contrastive
   – analysis 23f
   – grammar 25
   – phonetics 25

Danish
   – consonants 33f
   – intonation 118f
   – stops 39f
   – vowels 68f
dark [ɫ] 57f
declarative sentences 125, 126f
degree of raising, tongue height 63, 66
dental 32f
derivations
   vovel alternation 91
diphthongs 64, 66f, 83f
displaced articulation 15
distinctive feature 19f
distinctive function of accent 99
dynamic tonal prominence 98f, 107

echo questions 118, 127
elision 141
elliptical questions 127
enumeration 132
exclamations 126, 130
exclamatory questions 127

falling-rising tone groups 116f
falling tone groups 116f
feedback mechanism 11
final tone groups 131f
finishing intonation 131f
force of articulation
   with fricatives 47
   with stops 37
form, function words 94
fortis, strong
   – fricatives 47

– stops 38
free allophonic variant 19
fricatives 31f, 47f
   voiced and voiceless – 46f
front-closing diphthongs 66
front of tongue 13f
front vowels 63f, 66
functional classification 29
function, form words 94

glottal 32f
glottal plosive 45f
glottis 13
grammatical function of intonation 112
greetings 130
'groove-type' fricatives 31f

half-close vowels 63, 66f
half-open vowels 63, 66f
hard palate 13f
head 113f

ideographic, morphemic writing 27
imitation 23, 63
imperatives 125, 129f
interlinear tonetic transcription 98, 110
intonation 97, 110f
   attitudinal function of – 112
   continuing – 131f
   Danish – 118f
   finishing – 131f
   grammatical function of – 112
   language-specific – 112
   learning problems 119
   – and syntax 134f
   weaving pattern 120f
inventory of consonants 30f
inventory of vowels 65f
isochronous 109f

kindness/unkindness 116f, 125f

labial-velar 33, 59f
labiodental 32f
language-specific intonation 112
lateral 32
lateral release 36
larynx 12f
length of preceding sounds
   with fricatives 47
   with stops 37f
lenis, weak
   – fricatives 47
   – stops 38
lexical, content words 94
linguistic hierarchy 17
linking r 59
liquids 32, 57f
long
   – monophthongs 67, 71f
   – vowels 64, 67, 69f

machine-gun rhythm 110
main accent 99f
manner of articulation 14
   consonants 31f
minimal pair 18
modified breathing 12
monophthongs 64, 66f, 150
   long – 67, 71f
   short – 67, 75f
   weakening of – 90f
monosyllabic words
   vowel alternation 92f
morpheme 17
morphemic, ideographic writing 27
morse rhythm 110

nasal release 36
nasals 32, 55f
neutralisation 38f
neutral vowel 82, 90f
new topic 133
no accent 99f, 107f, 124
non-final tone groups 131f

non-lateral 32
non-linguistic features 97
non-phonemic assimilation 139
non-segmental 97
non-sibilants 31f
nucleus 113f
   – advancing 115f

obstruents 31f
open vowels 63, 66f
organs of speech 11f
orthography 27f

palatal 32f
palate 13f
palato-alveolar 32f
paralinguistic features 97
passive articulator 14
peak of prominence 113
peak of sonority 141
personal pronouns
   vowel alternation 93
pharynx 12f
phonation 12f, 32
   – system 13
phoneme 17f
phonemic, alphabetic writing 27
phonemic assimilation 139
phonetics
   acoustic – 11
   applied – 23f
   articulatory – 11
   auditory – 11
phonetic transcription 28
phrase 17
pitch 13, 110f
   new topic 133
pitch range 118
   – in Danish 121
place of articulation 14f
   assimilation 140
   consonants 33
   vowels 63, 66

plosives 31f
prefix rule 101
prepositions
    vowel alternation 93
primary accent 107f, 123f
progressive assimilation 139
prominence of syllables 97f
prosodic features 97
prosody 97f
phychological learning problems 119

quantity, vowel length 67, 69f
questions
    alternative – 132
    echo – 118, 127
    elliptical – 127
    exclamatory – 127
    statement – 127
    tag – 128f
    wh- – 125, 129
    yes-no – 125, 127f

regressive assimilation 139
reinforcement by glottal closure 46
relative clauses 134f
relative pitch 111
release stage 35f
reporting clauses 137
respiratory system 12
rhythm 109f
rhythmically conditioned accent 102
rhythmic variation 103f, 106
rising tone groups 116f
rounded vowels 64f, 67

secondary accent 107f, 123f
segmental 97
segmentation of speech 112f
semantically conditioned sentence
    accent 108f
semi-vowels 32, 59f
sentence 17

– accent 107f
– adverbials 135f
– rhythm 109f
short
    – monophthongs 67, 75f
    – vowels 64, 67, 69f, 75f
sibiliants 31f
simplified transcription 123f
'slit-type' fricatives 32
soft palate 13f
sonorants 31f
sonority 31, 141f
    – principle 142
sound substitution 24
speech channel 13
speed of articulation 109
springboard 113f
stability of articulation 66
stages of stops 35f
statement questions 127
static tonal prominence 98f, 107
stepping rise 118
'stød' 13, 46
stops 31f, 35f
    Danish – 39f
    voiced and voiceless – 37f
stress 98f, 107
subordinate tone group 132f
subsidiary accent 99f, 102f
suffix rule 101
syllabic
    – function 29
    – structure 142
    – writing 27
syllable 141f
syllable-timed rhythm 110
syntax
    intonation and – 134f
system of consonants 31f
system of vowels 66f

tag questions 128f
tail 113f
teaching of pronunciation 25f, 119f

tertiary accent 107f, 124
tip of tongue 13f
tonal
   – concord 134
   – prominence 98f, 107
tone 98
   – glide 113
   – languages 111
   – movement 98
tone group 113f
   – boundary 114
   final – 131f
   non-final – 131f
   subordinate – 132f
   – types 116f
tonetic
   – stress marks 123
   – transcription 98, 110f, 123f
tongue 13
tongue height, degree of raising 63, 66
transcription
   phonetic – 28
   simplified – 123f
   tonetic – 98, 110f, 123f

unaffricated stops 31f
unitary accent 104f
units of information 112f
unrounded vowels 64, 67
upward tone jump 115
use of tone-group types 116f, 125f
uvular r in Danish 59

velar 32f
velum 13f
verb + adverb compounds 105
vocal cords 13

vocatives 137
voice
   assimilation 140
voiced and voiceless
   – fricatives 46f
   – stops 37f
voiced consonants 32f
voiceless consonants 32f
voicing
   with fricatives 47
   with stops 37
vowel
   – alternation 90f
   – elision 141
vowel length, quantity 67, 69f
   – and accent 98, 107
   – variation 70
vowel quality and accent 98f, 107
vowels 29f, 63f
   Danish – 68f
   inventory of – 65f
   long – 64, 67, 69f
   rounding 64f, 67
   short – 64, 67, 69f, 75f
   system of – 66f
   – in unaccented syllables 90f
weakening of monophthongs 90f
weak forms 92f
weaving pattern 120f
wh-questions 125, 129
word accent 100f
word-class rule 102
word-external assimilation 139
word-internal assimilation 139
writing 27f

yes-no questions 125, 127f

Descriptions of individual phonemes

/p/	41	/iː/	71
/b/	41	/ɪ/	75
/t/	41	/e/	76
/d/	42	/æ/	77
/tʃ/	42	/ɑː/	72
/dʒ/	42	/ɒ/	79
/k/	44	/ɔː/	72
/g/	45	/ʊ/	81
/f/	47	/uː/	73
/v/	48	/ə/	82
/θ/	49	/ɜː/	74
/ð/	50	/ʌ/	78
/s/	51	/eɪ/	83
/z/	51	/aɪ/	84
/ʃ/	52	/ɔɪ/	85
/ʒ/	53	/əʊ/	86
/h/	54	/aʊ/	87
/m/	55	/ɪə/	88
/n/	56	/eə/	88
/ŋ/	56	/ʊə/	89
/l/	57		
/r/	58		
/w/	59		
/j/	60		